SONG OF
SOLOMON

Toni Morrison

EDITORIAL DIRECTOR Justin Kestler
EXECUTIVE EDITOR Ben Florman

SERIES EDITORS Boomie Aglietti, John Crowther, Justin Kestler
PRODUCTION Christian Lorentzen

WRITER Vladimir Kleyman
EDITORS Boomie Aglietti, Benjamin Morgan

This edition published by Spark Publishing

Spark Publishing
A Division of SparkNotes LLC
120 Fifth Avenue, 8th Floor
New York, NY 10011

02 03 04 05 SN 9 8 7 6 5 4 3 2 1

Please send all comments and questions or report errors to feedback@sparknotes.com.

Library of Congress information available upon request

Printed and bound in the United States

RRD-C

ISBN 1-58663-826-2

Introduction:
Stopping to Buy Sparknotes on a Snowy Evening

Whose words these are you *think* you know.
Your paper's due tomorrow, though;
We're glad to see you stopping here
To get some help before you go.

Lost your course? You'll find it here.
Face tests and essays without fear.
Between the words, good grades at stake:
Get great results throughout the year.

Once school bells caused your heart to quake
As teachers circled each mistake.
Use SparkNotes and no longer weep,
Ace every single test you take.

Yes, books are lovely, dark, and deep,
But only what you grasp you keep,
With hours to go before you sleep,
With hours to go before you sleep.

Contents

CONTEXT

TONI MORRISON WAS BORN Chloe Anthony Wofford on February 18, 1931, in Lorrain, Ohio, a steel town on the banks of Lake Erie. Morrison's parents, George and Rahmah, were children of sharecroppers who migrated from rural Georgia and Alabama. The second of four children, Morrison excelled in high school, graduated from Howard University, and received her master's degree from Cornell. Initially opting for a career as a teacher and editor, Morrison became an instructor at several historically black universities and worked for Random House. She brought writers such as Angela Davis and Toni Cade Bambara to national prominence. Morrison married and later divorced a Jamaican architect, Harold Morrison. The couple had two sons.

Morrison began her first novel, *The Bluest Eye*, while she taught at Howard University. It was published to critical acclaim in 1970. Morrison's second novel, *Sula*, brought the young author national recognition as well as a nomination for the 1975 National Book Award in fiction. *Song of Solomon*, Morrison's third novel, was popular with both critics and readers. In 1978, the novel won the National Critics Circle Award and the Letters Award. 570,000 paperback copies are currently in print. Morrison's carreer continued its meteoric rise, and in 1988 she won a Pulitzer Prize for her novel *Beloved*. In 1993, Toni Morrison joined the exclusive ranks of the world's premier writers when she became the first African-American woman to win the Nobel Prize in literature.

Morrison's fiction does not fit well into a single category. It blends themes of race and class, coming-of-age stories, and mythical and realistic genres. Some critics classify Morrison as magical realist in the vein of Gabriel García Márquez. However, others claim that she is a black classicist, an heir to nineteenth century European novelists such as Gustave Flaubert and Fyodor Dostoevsky. Finally, other scholars argue that African-American oral narratives, rather than European traditions, provide the raw material for her work. Morrison draws on all of these styles to create a rich tapestry of backgrounds and experiences for her distinctive characters.

Morrison's biography serves as rich source material for the literary characters in *Song of Solomon*. Jake (also known as Macon

Dead I) has experiences similar to those of Morrison's beloved grandfather, John Solomon Willis. After losing his land and being forced to become a sharecropper, Willis became disillusioned by the unfulfilled promises of the Emancipation Proclamation, Abraham Lincoln's 1865 document freeing black slaves. The character Heddy may have been modeled after Morrison's Native American great-grandmother. Guitar is a composite character, made up of Morrison's family and friends whose lives were destroyed by racism. Milkman's journey to uncover his roots can be compared to Morrison's own. Like Milkman's, Morrison's creative life began after age thirty and has been grounded in the African-American experience.

Toni Morrison has said in interviews that she opposed desegregation in the early 1960s despite being aware of its terrible effects. She worried that the excellent historically black schools and universities would disappear. Morrison wondered if the treasures of folklore, art, music, and literature created by the relatively insular African-American community would disappear once that community became more porous. Accordingly, while Song of Solomon explores the different experiences of white people and black people, almost all of the action occurs within an African-American world, drawing on its vitality for inspiration.

Although the black community provides the setting of Song of Solomon, the novel's themes are universal. Milkman's quest toward self-discovery, Macon Jr.'s obsession with wealth, Pilate's boundless love for others, Ryna's and Hagar's madness from broken hearts, and Guitar's destructive thirst for revenge are classic stories that have been told countless times in literatures of all traditions.

Plot Overview

ROBERT SMITH, AN INSURANCE AGENT in an unnamed Michigan town, leaps off the roof of Mercy Hospital wearing blue silk wings and claiming that he will fly to the opposite shore of Lake Superior. Mr. Smith plummets to his death. The next day, Ruth Foster Dead, the daughter of the first black doctor in town, gives birth to the first black child born in Mercy Hospital, Milkman Dead.

Discovering at age four that humans cannot fly, young Milkman loses all interest in himself and others. He grows up nourished by the love of his mother and his aunt, Pilate. He is taken care of by his sisters, First Corinthians and Magdalene (called Lena), and adored by his lover and cousin, Hagar. Milkman does not reciprocate their kindness and grows up bored and privileged. In his lack of compassion, Milkman resembles his father, Macon Dead II, a ruthless landlord who pursues only the accumulation of wealth.

Milkman is afflicted with a genetic malady, an emotional disease that has its origins in oppressions endured by past generations and passed on to future ones. Milkman's grandfather, Macon Dead, received his odd name when a drunk Union soldier erroneously filled out his documents (his grandfather's given name remains unknown to Milkman). Eventually, Macon was killed while defending his land. His two children, Macon Jr. and Pilate, were irreversibly scarred by witnessing the murder and became estranged from each other. Pilate has become a poor but strong and independent woman, the mother of a family that includes her daughter, Reba, and her granddaughter, Hagar. In contrast, Macon Jr. spends his time acquiring wealth. Both his family and his tenants revile him.

By the time Milkman reaches the age of thirty-two, he feels stifled living with his parents and wants to escape to somewhere else. Macon Jr. informs Milkman that Pilate may have millions of dollars in gold wrapped in a green tarp suspended from the ceiling of her rundown shack. With the help of his best friend, Guitar Bains, whom he promises a share of the loot, Milkman robs Pilate. Inside the green tarp, Milkman and Guitar find only some rocks and a human skeleton. We later learn that the skeleton is that of Milkman's grandfather, Macon Dead I. Guitar is especially disappointed not to find the gold because he needs the funds to carry out his mission for the Seven Days, a secret society that avenges injustices committed against African-Americans by murdering innocent whites.

Thinking that the gold might be in a cave near Macon's old Pennsylvania farm, Milkman leaves his hometown in Michigan and heads south, promising Guitar a share of whatever gold he finds. Before he leaves, Milkman severs his romantic relationship with Hagar, who is driven mad by his rejection and tries to kill Milkman on multiple occasions. After arriving in Montour County, Pennsylvania, Milkman discovers that there is no gold to be found. He looks for his long-lost family history rather than for gold. Milkman meets Circe, an old midwife who helped deliver Macon Jr. and Pilate. Circe tells Milkman that Macon's original name was Jake and that he was married to an Indian girl, Sing.

Encouraged by his findings, Milkman heads south to Shalimar, his grandfather's ancestral home in Virginia. Milkman does not know that he is being followed by Guitar, who wants to murder Milkman because he believes that Milkman has cheated him out of his share of the gold. While Milkman initially feels uncomfortable in Shalimar's small-town atmosphere, he grows to love it as he uncovers more and more clues about his family history. Milkman finds that Jake's father, his great-grandfather, was the legendary flying African, Solomon, who escaped slavery by flying back to Africa. Although Solomon's flight was miraculous, it left a scar on his family that has lasted for generations. After an unsuccessful attempt to take Jake, his youngest son, with him on the flight, Solomon abandoned his wife, Ryna, and their twenty-one children. Unable to cope without a husband, Ryna went insane, leaving Jake to be raised by Heddy, an Indian woman whose daughter, Sing, he married.

Milkman's findings give him profound joy and a sense of purpose. Milkman becomes a compassionate, responsible adult. After surviving an assassination attempt at Guitar's hands, Milkman returns home to Michigan to tell Macon Jr. and Pilate about his discoveries. At home, he finds that Hagar has died of a broken heart and that the emotional problems plaguing his family have not gone away. Nevertheless, Milkman accompanies Pilate back to Shalimar, where they bury Jake's bones on Solomon's Leap, the mountain from which Solomon's flight to Africa began. Immediately after Jake's burial, Pilate is struck dead by a bullet that Guitar had intended for Milkman. Heartbroken over Pilate's death but invigorated by his recent transformation, Milkman calls out Guitar's name and leaps toward him.

Character List

Milkman Dead The protagonist of the novel, also known as Macon Dead III. Born into a sheltered, privileged life, Milkman grows up to be an egotistical young man. He lacks compassion, wallows in self-pity, and alienates himself from the African-American community. As his nickname suggests, Milkman literally feeds off of what others produce. But his eventual discovery of his family history gives his life purpose. Although he remains flawed, this newfound purpose makes him compassionate and caring.

Pilate Dead Macon Jr.'s younger sister. Born without a navel, Pilate is physically and psychologically unlike the novel's other characters. She is a fearless mother who is selflessly devoted to others. Pilate is responsible for Milkman's safe birth and continues to protect him for years afterward. She also takes care of her daughter, Reba, and granddaughter, Hagar.

Macon Jr. Milkman's father and Ruth's husband, also known as Macon Dead II. Traumatized by seeing his father murdered during a skirmish over the family farm, Macon Jr. has developed an obsession with becoming wealthy. In the process, he has become an emotionally dead slumlord. His stony heart softens only when he reminisces about his childhood. Macon Jr.'s stories about his childhood help fuel Milkman's investigation into the history of the Dead family.

Guitar Bains Milkman's best friend. Having grown up in poverty after his father was killed in a factory accident, Guitar harbors a lifelong hatred for white people, whom he sees as responsible for all evil in the world. Morrison points out that while Guitar's rage is justifiable, his murders of white people neither combat racism nor help the African-American community.

Hagar   Pilate's daughter and Milkman's lover. Hagar devotes herself to Milkman, even though he loses interest and frequently rejects her. Like her biblical namesake—a servant who, after bearing Abraham's son is thrown out of the house by his barren wife, Sarah—Hagar is used and abandoned. Her plight demonstrates a central theme in *Song of Solomon*: the inevitable abandonment of women who love men too much.

Macon Dead I Macon Jr.'s father and Milkman's grandfather, Macon Dead I is also known as Jake. Macon Dead I was abandoned in infancy when his father, Solomon, flew back to Africa and his mother, Ryna, went insane. Macon Dead I was raised by an Indian woman, Heddy. The mysterious legend of his identity motivates Milkman's search for self-understanding.

Ruth Foster Dead Macon Jr.'s wife and the mother of Milkman, First Corinthians, and Lena. After growing up in a wealthy home, Ruth feels unloved by everyone except her deceased father, Dr. Foster. Although her existence is joyless, she refuses to leave Macon Jr. for a new life, proving that wealth's hold is difficult to overcome.

Dr. Foster The first black doctor in the novel's Michigan town. Dr. Foster is an arrogant, self-hating racist who calls fellow African-Americans "cannibals" and checks to see how light-skinned his granddaughters are when they are born. His status as an educated black man at a time when many blacks were illiterate makes him an important symbol of personal triumph while contrasting with his racist attitude.

Reba   Pilate's daughter and Hagar's mother, also known as Rebecca. Reba has a strong sexual drive but is attracted to abusive men. Nevertheless, because Pilate is her mother, the few men who dare mistreat her are punished. Reba's uncanny ability to win contests such as the Sears half-millionth customer diamond ring giveaway demonstrates that wealth is transient and unimportant.

First Corinthians Dead Milkman's worldly sister, educated at Bryn Mawr and in France. First Corinthians shares her name with a New Testament book in which the apostle Paul seeks to mend the disagreements within the early Christian church. Like the biblical book, the character First Corinthians tries to unify people. Her passionate love affair with a yardman, Henry Porter, crosses class boundaries. Her actions prove that human beings of different backgrounds and ages can share a bond.

Magdalene Dead Another of Milkman's sisters, also known as Lena. Lena's submissive attitude in Macon Jr.'s home makes her one of the many submissive women who populate *Song of Solomon*. But her rebuke of Milkman's selfishness demonstrates her inner strength.

Michael-Mary Graham The Michigan poet laureate. Graham is a liberal who writes sentimental poetry and hires First Corinthians as a maid. Graham represents the double standard of white liberals. Although they claimed to support universal human rights, liberal whites often refused to treat African-Americans as equals.

Circe A maid and midwife who worked for the wealthy Butler family. Circe delivered Macon Jr. and Pilate. In her encounter with Milkman, Circe plays the same role as her namesake in Homer's *Odyssey*, the ancient Greek account of a lost mariner's ten-year voyage home. Just as Homer's Circe helps Odysseus find his way back to Ithaca, Morrison's Circe provides crucial information that reconnects Milkman with his family history. In this way, Morrison's Circe connects Milkman's past and future.

Sing Milkman's grandmother and Macon Dead I's wife. Sing is an Indian woman also known as Singing Bird. Sing's name commands Macon Dead I, Pilate, and Milkman to connect the missing links of their family history through Solomon's song.

Henry Porter First Corinthians's lover and a member of the Seven Days vigilante group, which murders white people. Porter's tender love affair with First Corinthians proves that a personal connection between two human beings is stronger than differences of background and class.

Robert Smith An insurance agent and member of the Seven Days vigilante group. Smith's attempt to fly off of the roof of Mercy Hospital begins the novel's exploration of flight as a means of escape. Smith's failure to fly contrasts with Milkman's eventual success in escaping the confining circumstances of his life.

Freddie A janitor employed by Macon Jr. Freddie is the town gossip. Freddie spreads rumors through the town, illustrating how information was often disseminated within African-American communities. Freddie coins the nickname "Milkman" for Ruth's son, showing that original names are often forgotten and replaced.

Solomon Milkman's great-grandfather, who supposedly flew back to Africa but dropped his son Jake shortly after taking off. Solomon's flight is a physical demonstration of the liberation that is felt when a person escapes confining circumstances. However, Solomon's crying wife, Ryna, and traumatized children show that escape has negative consequences as well.

Ryna Milkman's great-grandmother and Solomon's wife. When Solomon abandons her, Ryna goes mad. According to legend, her cries can still be heard.

Sweet A prostitute with whom Milkman has a brief affair. Unlike Milkman's affairs with other women, especially Hagar, his relationship with Sweet is mutually respectful and entirely reciprocal. His interactions with her demonstrate that the most gratifying relationships in the novel are those in which both partners treat each other as equals.

ANALYSIS OF MAJOR CHARACTERS

MILKMAN DEAD

Milkman is considered the protagonist of the novel by critics who view *Song of Solomon* primarily as a coming-of-age story. Milkman is born into the noble lineage of a prominent black doctor and a wealthy landowner. He shares characteristics with heroes ranging from Odysseus, in Homer's *Odyssey,* to Holden Caulfield, in J.D. Salinger's *The Catcher in the Rye.* Both Odysseus and Milkman search for their ancestral homes. And like Holden Caulfield, Milkman makes his most important journey inside his soul as he grows from an egotistical young man into a compassionate adult.

Prior to this transformation, Milkman is a selfish young man who lacks any consideration for others. Although he fits in at upscale parties, Milkman feels alienated by his family, other African-Americans of all classes, and humanity in general. He is also physically different from the people around him, since he has an undersized leg. Since Milkman is able to conceal his leg, he believes that he can also hide his emotional shortcomings. Other characters, however, are aware of Milkman's oddities. His mother's guests comment that he is a strange child and his schoolmates frequently tease him and beat him. Even when Milkman is a grown man, his behavior is much different from that of the rest of his community. He even walks against the flow of traffic on the street. Although Milkman is flawed, his family loves him unconditionally. Milkman does not return their love, and causes them much pain.

Milkman's distorted personality is not entirely his fault. Morrison shows us that generations of slavery and abuse have played a part in developing Milkman's selfish personality. Milkman's immaturity stems directly from the enslavement and ensuing escape of his great-grandfather, Solomon. Because Solomon escaped, Milkman's grandfather, Macon Dead I, grew up an orphan. In turn, Macon Dead I's son, Macon Jr., witnesses white men murder his father. Macon Jr. never fully recovers from witnessing his father's death; he becomes a greedy, vicious man who raises his own son, Milkman, to share those characteristics. The racism that has afflicted Milkman's ancestors is partially responsible for Milkman's own selfishness. Milkman is finally able to heal his wounds by traveling to Shalimar, the site of Solomon's flight toward liberty.

PILATE DEAD

Pilate can also be seen as the protagonist of *Song of Solomon* because she is the novel's moral guide. Although the narrator rarely focuses on what Pilate is feeling or thinking, preferring instead to concentrate on Milkman's quest, Pilate's presence is felt everywhere in the novel. Despite being named after the Roman statesman who, according to the New Testament, ordered Jesus' crucifixion, Pilate is completely incapable of cruelty. It is more accurate to see her name as a homonym for "pilot." She is frequently leading someone who is in need of guidance, such as the skeleton of her dead father, or Milkman, during his spiritual journey.

Although Pilate's actions in the novel are less visible than Milkman's, her role is just as important. Born without a navel and alienated from others, Pilate is a survivor of the same racism that has embittered Macon Jr. and Milkman. Pilate is nevertheless loving and selfless. Her one regret when dying is that she could not have loved more people. Pilate's loving nature does not connote weakness but rather strength. When a man beats her daughter, Reba, Pilate pushes a knife within an inch of his heart and persuades him never to touch Reba again. Even though she is in her sixties and Reba's abuser is a strong young man, Pilate prevails.

Morrison suggests that Pilate's supernatural powers, great strength, lasting youthfulness, and boundless love come from African-American cultural traditions. Although Pilate suffers the same disadvantages as Macon Jr., she is still able to preserve a link to her family's forgotten past. By singing folk songs about Sugarman's flight, Pilate recreates a past in which her ancestors shed the yoke of oppression. Her recreation of this past sustains the characters who live in the present. Both Macon Jr., who secretly eavesdrops on her nightly singing sessions, and Milkman, who uses the songs to find his ancestral home, Shalimar, need Pilate to keep alive the remaining vestiges of their humanity. Indeed, as Milkman realizes at the end of his journey, Pilate is the only human being he knows who is able to fly without ever leaving the ground. That is, she is already liberated and does not need to escape to attain freedom. Ultimately, Pilate becomes the novel's model character, showing that strength does not have to come at the expense of gentleness, and that personal freedom is not necessarily compromised by love for others.

RUTH FOSTER DEAD

Unlike Pilate, who is strong-willed, Ruth is a subdued, quiet, upper-class woman. Ruth relies on Pilate for financial support. As a result, Ruth never develops into a strongly independent person. Until age sixteen, she was cared for by her father, Dr. Foster. After she married Macon Jr., he took care of her. Because she considers giving birth to Milkman her life accomplishment, some critics argue that Ruth represents the unliberated woman whose own goals are dictated by a sexist society.

However, Ruth does not always submit to the will of men. Ruth is less assertive than Pilate, but she exercises her will in more subtle ways. For instance, while Ruth was pregnant with Milkman, she and Pilate collaborated to ensure his safe birth despite the efforts of Macon Jr., who tried to force Ruth to abort the child. Pilate threatened Macon Jr. directly by storming into his office and leaving an impaled voodoo doll in his chair. Ruth's evasion of Macon Jr. was more subtle. When Macon Jr. forced Ruth to stick needles into her womb in order to damage the fetus, she only partially inserted them, ensuring that Milkman remained unharmed. Furthermore, despite Macon Jr.'s seething anger over Ruth's affection for her father, Ruth continues to visit his grave frequently. Her subtle independence makes her a foil for Pilate.

THEMES, MOTIFS & SYMBOLS

THEMES

Themes are the fundamental and often universal ideas explored in a literary work.

FLIGHT AS A MEANS OF ESCAPE

The epigraph to *Song of Solomon*—"The fathers may soar / And the children may know their names"—is the first reference to one of the novel's most important themes. While flight can be an escape from constricting circumstances, it also scars those who are left behind. Solomon's flight allowed him to leave slavery in the Virginia cotton fields, but it also meant abandoning his wife, Ryna, with twenty-one children. While Milkman's flight from Michigan frees him from the dead environment of Not Doctor Street, his flight is also selfish because it causes Hagar to die of heartbreak. The novel's epigraph attempts to break the connection between flight and abandonment. Because Pilate, as Milkman notes, is able to fly without ever lifting her feet off the ground, she has mastered flight, managing to be free of subjugation without leaving anyone behind.

Morrison's extensive use of flying as a literal and not just metaphorical event pushes *Song of Solomon* toward the genre of magical realism. The novel's characters accept human flight as natural. For instance, the observers of Robert Smith's flight encourage him rather than rush to prevent his leap, implying that they do not see his flight as a suicide attempt. Instead, the onlookers behave as though Smith's flight might be possible. Furthermore, the residents of Shalimar, Virginia, do not think that Solomon's flight is a myth; they believe that the flight actually occurred. Morrison's novel belongs to the genre of magical realism because in it human flight is both possible and natural. For the long period of time during which Milkman doubts the possibility of human flight, he remains abnormal in the eyes of his community. Only when he begins to believe in the reality of flight does he cease to feel alienated.

THEMES

ABANDONED WOMEN

Men's repeated abandonment of women in *Song of Solomon* shows that the novel's female characters suffer a double burden. Not only are women oppressed by racism, but they must also pay the price for men's freedom. Guitar tells Milkman that black men are the unacknowledged workhorses of humanity, but the novel's events imply that black women more correctly fit this description. The scenes that describe women's abandonment show that in the novel, men bear responsibility only for themselves, but women are responsible for themselves, their families, and their communities. For instance, after suffering through slavery, Solomon flew home to Africa without warning anyone of his departure. But his wife, Ryna, who was also a slave, was forced to remain in Virginia to raise her twenty-one children alone. Also, after Guitar's father is killed in a factory accident, Guitar's grandmother has to raise him and his siblings. Although she is elderly and ill, she supports her children financially, intellectually, and emotionally.

Relying on this skewed idea of gender roles, the society in the novel judges men and women differently. While men who fly away from their communities and families are venerated as heroes, women who do the same are judged to be irresponsible. Although Solomon abandoned his family with his flight to Africa, generations later he is remembered as the brave patriarch of the whole community. At the same time, Ryna, who was left to care for a brood of children, is remembered as a woman who went mad because she was too weak to uphold her end of the bargain. Residents of Shalimar have named a scary, dark gulch after Ryna, while they have given Solomon's name to a scenic mountain peak. The community rewards Solomon's abandonment of his children but punishes Ryna's inability to take care of them alone.

THE ALIENATING EFFECTS OF RACISM

Racism is the central cause of suffering in the novel. Racism has long-lasting damaging effects on the community. Slavery causes Solomon to flee toward freedom and end his marriage to Ryna. This flight begins many generations of trauma. The knowledge that his father died because of his white employers' negligence makes Guitar especially sensitive to the injustices perpetrated against African-Americans. Emmett Till's murder and the Birmingham Church bombing remind Guitar of his own tragedy, transforming him into a ruthless, vengeful murderer. Guitar's story shows that racism alienates its victims from their native communities and causes them to lose touch with their own humanity.

MOTIFS

Motifs are recurring structures, contrasts, or literary devices that can help to develop and inform the text's major themes.

BIBLICAL ALLUSIONS

Song of Solomon's title refers to the biblical book of the same name, emphasizing that the novel adresses age-old themes. The biblical book depicts a conversation between two lovers, King Solomon and his beautiful, black Shulamite bride. Similarly, Morrison's novel is a celebration of the triumph of earthly love. Morrison gives her characters biblical names in order to align them with well-known figures. As a result, many of the characters in *Song of Solomon* carry with them not only their own personal history as described in the novel, but also the history of a biblical namesake. By giving her characters the names of biblical figures, Morrison compares them to epic heroes whose experience transcends cultural and temporal boundaries. For instance, the biblical Hagar is Sarah's handmaiden, who bears Sarah's husband Abraham a son and is then banished from his sight. Likewise, Morrison's Hagar is used by Milkman, who enjoys her offerings. The similarity of both Hagars' experiences suggests that women will be abused in any patriarchal society.

NAMES

In *Song of Solomon,* names show the effects of both oppression and liberation. Before Milkman uncovers his grandfather's true name, he is known as Macon Dead, the same name that white oppressors gave his grandfather. When Milkman finds out his grandfather's true name he begins to feel proud of himself and his family. The fact that Milkman's nickname describes him better than his recorded name shows that written names are often unreliable. For this reason, they are often replaced by names from the oral tradition. For instance, Dr. Foster's street is officially labeled Mains Avenue. But after his death, it is commonly known as "Not Doctor Street." Although the official name is accurate, the popular name is more descriptive.

In the novel, names describe characters' personalities and behavior. Circe, for instance, shares her name with an enchantress in

Homer's *Odyssey* who provides Odysseus with crucial help for his voyage homeward. Likewise, Morrison's Circe directs Milkman toward his ancestral home and allows him to bridge a gap in his family history. Another example is Guitar's last name, Bains, which is a homonym for "banes," or sources of distress. His name suggests both the oppression he has suffered and his profession as an assassin. Finally, Pilate's name is a homonym for "pilot." She guides Milkman along his journey to spiritual redemption.

SINGING

In *Song of Solomon,* singing is a means of maintaining a link to a forgotten family history. In a community where most of the past generations were illiterate, songs rather than history books tell the story of the past. Songs record details about Milkman's heritage and cause Milkman to research his family history. Pilate's songs about Sugarman, for instance, encourage Milkman's quest to Virginia. Similarly, the songs Milkman hears about Solomon and Ryna inform him of the mysterious fate of his ancestors, and keep him on the path to self-discovery.

Milkman is not the only character who is guided by song. Other members of the Dead family use songs and singing to heal themselves spiritually and emotionally. When Macon Jr. is depressed, for example, he secretly listens to Pilate's songs under her windows. Similarly, after Hagar dies, both Pilate and Reba cope with their grief by singing a mighty rendition of a gospel tune. The healing power of song is a common theme in African-American culture, where it brings people together and allows people to share experiences.

SYMBOLS

Symbols are objects, characters, figures, or colors used to represent abstract ideas or concepts.

WHITENESS

Almost all of the characters in *Song of Solomon* are black. The few white characters represent violence and wrongdoing. After Guitar's father is cut in half during a sawmill accident, for example, the mill's white foreman offers the family almost no sympathy or financial support. Likewise, Circe's wealthy white employers, the Butlers, are murderers. When they take Macon Dead I's land, they end his children's innocence. Even white animals carry negative connotations.

A white bull causes Freddie's mother to go into labor and die. The bull's interference with Freddie's birth represents white people's devastating interference with the African-American world. Likewise, the white peacock that causes Guitar and Milkman to become infatuated with the pursuit of wealth represents the corrupting influence of greed.

ARTIFICIAL ROSES

First Corinthians and Lena make artificial roses that represent the stifling life of the upper class and the oppression of women. The roses do not bring in much money; the true purpose of the activity is to provide a mindless distraction from their boredom. First Corinthians and Lena perform their task without any enthusiasm, motivated by habit rather than conviction. In literary works, living roses often symbolize love. The artificial roses sybolize the absence of love in Macon Jr.'s household. Unlike living plants, the artificial flowers convey only the depression of their makers.

GOLD

Gold represents Macon Jr.'s obsessive pursuit of wealth. Gold is utterly irresistible to men in the novel, who violate their principles in order to get it. For example, Milkman robs his aunt, Pilate, because he wants to be wealthy and independent. Likewise, Guitar's desire for gold motivates his attempted murder of Milkman. Finally, Macon Jr. spends a lifetime pursuing gold without any greater goal beyond accumulation.

SYMBOLS

Summary & Analysis

Chapter 1

Her head cocked to one side, her eyes fixed on Mr.
Robert Smith, she sang in a powerful contralto.

(See QUOTATIONS, p. 55)

Summary

On Wednesday, February 18, 1931, Robert Smith, a North Carolina Mutual Life insurance agent, teeters atop Mercy Hospital in an unnamed Michigan town. Wearing blue silk wings and promising to fly off the hospital roof, the formerly nondescript insurance agent draws a crowd of forty or fifty mostly African-American town residents. Mercy Hospital, known as "No Mercy Hospital" among locals because it does not admit blacks, stands at the end of a street called "Mains Avenue" by the post office but commonly labeled "Not Doctor Street." The street received its nickname from the fact that a black physician, Dr. Foster, once lived and practiced there.

As Robert Smith prepares to fly off the roof, Dr. Foster's pregnant daughter, Ruth Foster Dead, stands in the crowd below with her two "half-grown" daughters, Magdalene ("Lena") Dead, and First Corinthians Dead. Ruth suddenly goes into labor. Dressed in an expensive gray coat with a black bow and four-button ladies' galoshes, Ruth clearly belongs to a higher economic class than the other, shabbily dressed spectators, who include her sister-in-law, Pilate Dead. Wrapped in an old quilt instead of a coat, Pilate fixes her eyes on Robert Smith and sings, "O Sugarman done fly away." Also present in the crowd is an elderly woman with several grandchildren, one of whom is a smart six-year-old named Guitar Bains. When a white nurse who orders Guitar to get the security guard from the hospital's admissions desk incorrectly spells the word "admissions" out loud, Guitar catches her mistake.

Eventually, Mr. Smith leaps off the hospital roof and Ruth Dead becomes Mercy Hospital's first black patient. The next day she gives birth to a son, Macon Dead III, who, at age four, discovers that only birds and airplanes can fly. He loses all interest in himself, becoming a "peculiar" child with deep, mysterious eyes. Ruth and her children live in Dr. Foster's enormous, twelve-room house, where they are isolated from love and abused by Ruth's husband, Macon Dead II. To escape the boredom of her sexless marriage, Ruth indulges in small, secret pleasures: polishing a watermark on her dining room table and breast-feeding her son long past infancy. When Freddie, the janitor, observes one of Ruth's breast-feeding sessions, he dubs her son "Milkman," a name that stays with him for the rest of his life.

The narrator tells us that Milkman's father, Macon Dead II (or Macon Jr.), is a ruthless slumlord, obsessed with accumulating wealth. He inherited his name from his illiterate father, Macon Dead I, whose own name came about when a drunk Union soldier incorrectly filled out an identity card. Every day, Macon Jr. sits in his real estate office, called Sonny's Shop by the tenants, squeezing the last dollars from his customers. When Guitar Bains's grandmother asks Macon Jr. to defer her rent payment in order for her to be able to feed her young grandchildren, he refuses without hesitation. In another instance, Macon Jr. finds out that one of his tenants, Henry Porter, has gotten drunk and is threatening to shoot himself. Instead of attempting to save Porter's life, he visits him to collect rent.

In his spare time, Macon Jr. reads his account books and reflects upon his family's history. He recalls the death of his mother, Ruth, while she was in labor, and the subsequent appearance of his younger sister, Pilate, who climbed out of her mother's womb without a navel. Pilate's name, like those of other children in the Dead family except for the firstborn sons, was picked blindly from the Bible. Macon Jr. parted with Pilate when he was seventeen and she was twelve and did not see her again until a year before Milkman's birth. Macon Jr. bans Pilate from his household, because he is ashamed of her unkempt appearance. He is also ashamed of her former career as a smuggler, her residence in a slum without electricity or running water, and her general disdain for material goods. But walking home on the night of Porter's attempted suicide, he is driven to stop by her house. Hiding in the shadows of her yard, Macon Jr. listens to Pilate, her daughter Rebecca (called "Reba"), and her young granddaughter, Hagar, sing a beautiful melody.

ANALYSIS

The first chapter of *Song of Solomon* sets the stage for the rest of the novel and points out its central elements: the theme of flight; the complex interplay of class, race, and gender; and the significance of names. The opening story of Robert Smith's disastrous death sets up the experiences of the novel's other characters. Much like Smith's flight, these other characters' quests to escape confining circumstances are generally doomed to fail. For example, Ruth Foster Dead's sole diversion from Macon's oppression is cut short when Freddie discovers her breast-feeding Milkman. Similarly, poor African-Americans, such as Henry Porter and Guitar Bains's family, are stuck in poverty, just as Macon Jr. is trapped by his wealth. Though Macon Jr. spends his days accumulating profit and wielding his power, his only moment of spiritual relief occurs in hiding, when he cowers under Pilate's windows. Finally, Mercy Hospital's unmerciful rejection of black patients and the white nurse's haughty attitude toward Guitar show that in addition to their individual problems, all the characters face racism everday.

Compared to Robert Smith's drastic leap, however, the other characters' attempts to escape seem feeble. Unlike Smith, who is unwilling to tolerate his circumstances any longer, these other characters accept the futility of trying to change their lives. For example, Milkman becomes bored with life when he realizes at age four that humans cannot physically fly. Likewise, Ruth Foster Dead tolerates her submissive role in the household and never lifts her voice against Macon Jr. Similarly, Lena and First Corinthians Dead show no signs of rebellion, preferring to spend their time quietly making artificial roses. Pilate Dead appears to be the only liberated character. Unburdened by material goods and unashamed of her poverty, she is the only one of Smith's spectators who refuses to be a passive observer. She answers Mr. Smith's flight with the power of her own will. She looks him in the eye and sings at the top of her voice.

The idea of human flight to freedom is rooted in both African-American and European literary traditions. Mr. Smith reminds us of Icarus, a human from Greek mythology who uses wings made out of wax in an attempt to fly close to the sun. Like Icarus, Smith plummets to his doom when his wings fail to carry him. Smith's flight also evokes a traditional Gullah folk tale about slaves who overcome subjugation in Southern cotton plantations by flying back to Africa. By alluding to two great literary narratives in the description of Robert Smith's failed flight, Morrison endows the flight with an epic quality that sets the stage for Milkman's eventual, successful flight.

The rest of the first chapter introduces us to the novel's characters and the inner conflicts that drive them. In the dim-witted nurse's bossing around of six-year-old Guitar Bains we see the origins of the adult Guitar's hatred for whites. Similarly, the glimpse of Macon Jr. privately basking in Pilate's simple song hints that he has a sensitive side beneath his hard, dead shell. Finally, that Ruth is well dressed, in contrast to the shabbily dressed crowd, suggests that Ruth is alienated from her fellow African-Americans and wants to become white. But her desire to be white meets resistance, as the white Mercy Hospital admits her only with great reluctance. Like her biblical namesake, Ruth the Moabite, who becomes estranged from her native people and struggles for acceptance among the Hebrews, Ruth Foster Dead is an outsider in both the black community and the white community.

Morrison's emphasis on names and naming suggests that the novel is ultimately about recovering and accepting lost identity. Macon Jr. is as spiritually dead as Milkman is after age four. But we know that "Macon Dead" is not the real name of any of the three Macons. This name is the result of an accident—a drunken Union soldier's shaky handwriting—which suggests that either of the living Macons (Macon Jr. and Milkman) can recover his true name and identity with a little bit of effort. Indeed, only when Milkman, on a journey to discover his lost family history, learns Macon Dead I's given name, can he begin to come to terms with his own identity.

Furthermore, names of geographic locations sometimes serve as milestones along Milkman's journey. For instance, Milkman's own street, dubbed Mains Avenue by the post office, is called "Not Doctor Street" by town residents—a more descriptive name, since a doctor who once lived there no longer does. Living on a street whose true name has been obscured by its nickname invites Milkman to question his own name, and spurs his quest toward self-discovery.

CHAPTER 2

It was becoming a habit—this concentration on things behind him. Almost as though there were no future to be had. (See QUOTATIONS, p. 56)

SUMMARY

The Dead family goes for a ride in their shiny, new, green Packard to the Honoré beach community, where Macon Jr. plans to build upscale summer homes for wealthy African-Americans. Macon Jr. drives the car through Not Doctor Street and through the rough part of town, known as the Blood Bank, where many of his tenants live.

Unlike the junk cars kept by poor Blood Bank residents, Macon Jr.'s Packard has never run out of gas, broken down in the middle of the street, or carried teenagers on its running boards. In fact, Macon Jr. keeps his car in such good condition that other blacks call it a "hearse" and stare at the automobile with a mixture of envy and mockery. In the middle of their trip, the young Milkman throws a temper tantrum and demands to use the bathroom. At first Macon Jr. ignores Milkman's requests and makes nasty comments about Ruth, but eventually he pulls over and Lena accompanies Milkman into the trees. While urinating, Milkman hears the sound of Lena's footsteps behind him and turns around before he is through, wetting his sister's pale-blue dress. The narrator tells us that concentrating on things behind him becomes a habit for Milkman, as though he does not have a future to look forward to.

At age twelve, in sixth grade, Milkman meets and becomes friends with Guitar Bains, an older, more mature high schooler. One day, Milkman follows Guitar to Pilate's house, despite Macon Jr.'s explicit prohibition against doing so. When Milkman sees Pilate for the first time, he is struck by her tall, powerful appearance. Although she is unkempt, she does not seem dirty, and her fingernails are as white as ivory. When Milkman asks Pilate if she is his father's sister, Pilate mysteriously responds that there "ain't but three Deads alive."

Pilate invites Milkman and Guitar into her home, which is decorated with a moss-green sack hanging from the ceiling, and makes them a soft-boiled egg. She then tells Milkman about how she and Macon Jr. were raised on a farm in Montour County, Pennsylvania, and that their father was shot while sitting on the fence, waiting for someone. After Macon Dead I's death, Pilate claims, she and Macon Jr. wandered the countryside and once saw their father's ghost sitting on a stump in the sunlight, an experience that left them shaking like leaves.

Pilate's narrative is interrupted by the arrival of her sixteen-year-old granddaughter, Hagar, with whom Milkman instantly falls in love, before even seeing her face. Pilate introduces Milkman as Hagar's brother, even though he is her cousin, saying that one has to act the same to both. Pilate's daughter, Reba, then shows the boys a diamond ring she won for being Sears Roebuck's half-millionth customer and tells them that she has a knack for winning things, like the ring and a hundred pounds of free groceries. Pilate and Reba ask Hagar if she has ever had a hungry day in her life, and when Hagar answers affirmatively, Pilate and Reba are brought to the verge of tears. They tell Hagar that they will get her anything she ever wants. Finally, Pilate, Reba, and Hagar sing in a chorus about Sugarman, who flies home across the sky—the same song that Pilate sang on the day of Robert Smith's flight.

Milkman leaves Pilate's home enchanted with Hagar and returns to Not Doctor Street to face his angry father. Macon Jr. questions Milkman about his forbidden visit to Pilate's place, but when Milkman asks about the death of Macon Dead I, Macon Jr. recalls that something "wild ran through him" when Macon Dead I died. He calms down and begins to reminisce about his childhood. With the same smile that Pilate wears while remembering Montour County, Macon Jr. recalls life on their farm, Lincoln's Heaven, for the first time in years. The narrator tells us that the previous time Macon Jr. told stories about his childhood was when he was still poor, just starting out in business, and first married to Ruth. Macon Jr. also tells Milkman how his father received his eccentric name. But when Milkman asks Macon Jr. to tell him Macon Dead I's real name, Macon Jr. ignores the question, remarking that his own mother was a light-skinned woman. Macon Jr. concludes his conversation with Milkman by reiterating his prohibition against visiting Pilate, who he claims is a treacherous "snake" who might be able to teach Milkman a few things in the next world, but not in this one. Macon Jr. also promises to introduce Milkman to the real estate business.

ANALYSIS

During the car ride to Honoré it becomes evident that even as a boy Milkman has inherited his father's ugly personality. It is fitting that Macon Jr., the haughty, emotionally dead landowner, drives around in a car labeled a "hearse." Having surely earned numerous enemies during his ruthless climb to the top, it would be logical for Macon Jr. to be wary of his surroundings. Instead, we find out that the paranoid Dead in the family is Milkman. His accidental urination on Lena shows that he is uncannily aware of everything behind him, both physically and metaphorically. Milkman's fear of the past even though he is not old enough to have much of a past suggests that the trauma of his father's and grandfather's pasts haunts him from birth. His belief that he has no future to look forward to implies that he is headed down Macon Jr.'s path toward spiritual death.

Just as Milkman has inherited a spiritual burden from Macon Jr., so has Macon Jr. inherited a spiritual burden from Macon Dead I.

The source of Macon Jr.'s bitterness seems to be the murder of his father, after which something "wild ran" inside him. His fanatical attachment to all material possessions, which developed after he saw his father die while defending his property, has alienated Macon Jr. from his own family and from humanity as a whole. But Morrison hints that Macon Dead I's murder is only a piece of the puzzle concerning Macon Jr. After all, even after his father's demise, while he was just starting out as a businessmen, Macon Jr. was still able to have heart-to-heart talks about his childhood with other men and with Ruth. Macon Jr.'s deadness, then, results also from the constant, numbing pursuit of material wealth and from a certain, unknown burden inherited from his own father, similar to the spiritual burden that Milkman has inherited from Macon Jr.

Whatever the cause of Macon Jr.'s spiritual ugliness, it is clear that Pilate is full of vitality and is somehow able to coax life even out of Macon Jr.'s stony heart. Just as in the first chapter, when we observe Macon Jr. cower under Pilate's windows, we catch a rare glimpse of Macon Jr.'s nearly destroyed humanity when he reminisces about Pilate. In contrast to his usually dour appearance, Macon Jr. smiles and laughs when he recalls growing up with Pilate in beautiful Lincoln's Heaven. Pilate has a similar effect on Milkman. Only after Milkman meets Pilate does he become curious about his family history and begin to ask Macon Jr. questions. Pilate's influence thus results in the first open conversation Macon Jr. has with Milkman, and helps crack Macon Jr.'s alienating shell.

Perhaps the best clues regarding the trauma haunting the Dead family can be found by comparing Pilate's and Macon Jr.'s memories of their childhood. While their recollections of Lincoln's Heaven are nearly identical, Macon Jr. notably omits the meeting with Macon Dead I's ghost. Both Pilate and Macon Jr. continue to be haunted by their father's death, but in telling Milkman about the ghostly encounter, Pilate shows a willingness to admit that the trauma is ongoing. Macon Jr., on the other hand, is unable or unwilling to admit this fact. His deliberate refusal to reveal Macon Dead I's original name to Milkman further suggests that he too is wrestling with the damage inflicted upon his father's identity. What Macon Jr. does not tell Milkman, then, is as important a key to understanding his emotional turmoil as what he willingly reveals.

The relationship that develops between Milkman and Hagar proves important as a measure of Milkman's maturity. Pilate's assertion that Milkman is Hagar's brother invites us to compare their relationship with that between the two lovers in the biblical Song of Solomon, from which Morrison takes the title for her novel. In the biblical story, the female is called both the male's "sister" and "bride." But the "sister" designation does not imply that the woman is the man's actual sibling; rather, she is his equal in their love. Consequently, within the context of Morrison's novel, Pilate's statement that Milkman is Hagar's brother may be a reminder to Milkman that he should treat Hagar with respect, as his equal. His mistreatment of her in subsequent chapters demonstrates that he is not yet mature enough to appreciate her love. He takes her love without giving, selfishly caring only for his own needs.

CHAPTER 3

The street was even more crowded with people, all going in the direction he was coming from.
(See QUOTATIONS, p. 57)

SUMMARY
At age twelve, Milkman begins to work for Macon Jr., which gives him an opportunity to spend more time on the Southside with Guitar, Pilate, and Hagar. Sometimes Milkman and Guitar visit a barbershop run by Railroad Tommy and Hospital Tommy, and listen to the older men discuss the racial inequality prevalent in 1940s America. After one of the discussions, Guitar confides to Milkman that his father was killed in a sawmill accident, an incident that left him angry at his father's white boss and white people in general.

At age fourteen, one of Milkman's legs grows shorter than the other and he masks the defect with a strut. As he grows older, Milkman does everything he can to dispel the town-dwellers' commonly shared belief that he is identical to his father. He acts like Macon Jr.'s opposite, growing facial hair, smoking cigarettes, and carelessly spending money when he can. When Milkman is twenty-two, his father hits his mother after a dinner table argument. Milkman retaliates by striking his father back. He promises to kill him if he is ever violent toward Ruth again, and struts upstairs to his bedroom. Macon Jr. follows him there and explains that there are reasons for his anger at Ruth. According to Macon Jr., Ruth's father, Dr. Foster, was a greedy, self-hating, bitter man who despised his son-in-law and called fellow African-Americans "cannibals." Furthermore, Macon Jr. claims that even though Dr. Foster was impotent, he may have had a sexual relationship with Ruth. Macon Jr. also tells Milkman that on the day of Dr. Foster's death, he saw Ruth lying naked next to her father's corpse, his fingers in her mouth.

Distraught by his father's revelations, Milkman goes to see Guitar. Along the way, he remembers being breast-fed by his mother beyond infancy and feels disturbed. He also realizes that his motivation for striking his father was not love for his mother, and comes to the sudden conclusion that his mother has a personal life outside of being his mother. As he is walking, Milkman notices that he is heading against the flow of other foot traffic.

Milkman finds Guitar at Tommy's Barbershop discussing two recently murdered boys: Emmet Till, a black Northerner killed in Mississippi, and a white boy killed in their town. Guitar speaks passionately about the injustices brought upon African-Americans and the need to correct them. He eventually leaves with Milkman. While they sit in a bar, Milkman tells Guitar about striking his father, and Guitar explains that the "cards are stacked against" black men, and that sometimes blacks are even coerced into hurting each other. Guitar then tries to compare Milkman's experience with Till's recent death, but Milkman is not interested in hearing about the murdered black boy, dismissing him as crazy. As he later ponders his life, Milkman realizes that everything bores him: money, the city, politics, and the racial problems that consume other African-Americans.

ANALYSIS

In this chapter, Morrison exposes the continual tension between Milkman's blistering arrogance and his awareness of his own failings. Though he is simultaneously alienated from his family, his best friend, and other African-Americans, Milkman continues to believe that the entire world revolves around him. Though he is privately insecure about his own shortcomings, such as his oddly short leg, Milkman also thinks that others, especially women, consider him a gift from God. On the surface, these beliefs seem contradictory. By turning Milkman into a complex character who is at odds with himself, however, Morrison makes his quest for self-understanding all the more difficult and rewarding.

Milkman's selfish worldview is nurtured by others' confirmations of his superiority, giving him no pressing reason to explore his own identity. Female affection and affirmation are readily available to him: he can decide on a whim whether he will sleep with Hagar. Similarly, Ruth also gives her love to him freely. Furthermore, while most African-Americans live in a world of daily discrimination and fear, Milkman knows only a life of luxury. Milkman is an optimist and his attitudes sometimes whitewash tragic events. He claims that the murdered black boy, Emmett Till, was crazy and feels the boy's plight is irrelevant to his own welfare. And though Milkman strikes his father, supposedly to defend his mother, he privately realizes that his action was entirely self-serving. He did it to prove his manhood, not because he loves Ruth. Milkman even takes advantage of Guitar, his best friend. He spills out his emotional turmoil to Guitar but refuses to devote an equal amount of time to hear about Guitar's internal struggle. Unaware that his behavior is hurtful to others, Milkman is content to live in a careless, egotistical manner.

Milkman's friends and family validate his arrogant behavior, which makes his quest to understand himself more difficult. Milkman is used to viewing himself as the center of the universe, and he is thus devastated when he understands that Ruth had and continues to have a life outside of being his mother. But the image of Milkman walking in a crowded street against the flow of traffic confirms his individuality. While this action represents Milkman's detachment from problems that concern his community and the world at large, it also indicates that he is beginning to fight against his irrelevance by starting down the path to maturity. As he proceeds against the flow, Milkman understands for the first time just how alienated he is—an important milestone in his quest for self-discovery.

The difference between Guitar and Milkman, which becomes apparent during their conversation at the bar, foreshadows the growing tension and hostility between the two friends. Although the open hatred that develops between them is a decade away, Morrison shows that Milkman and Guitar are divided by their different upbringings and worldviews. Milkman, who has led a life of privilege and belongs to the 1950s-era black upper class, is blind to pervasive white racism, protected from it by his luxurious life. Guitar, who lives in poverty brought about by his father's death at the hands of negligent white factory owners, sees everything through the lens of racial conflict. He sees oppression in every direction he looks, and is thus unable to draw a distinction between Emmett Till's murder and Milkman's argument with Macon Jr. Guitar's hostile attitude toward the world cannot coexist with Milkman's boredom, and we sense here that a conflict between the two friends is inevitable.

CHAPTER 4

SUMMARY

Over the years, Milkman's love for Hagar blooms and wilts. When he is seventeen and she is twenty-two, Hagar invites him into her room for the first time and makes love to him. For three years, Hagar teases Milkman with intermittent passion, sometimes accepting his advances, sometimes declining them. But by the time Milkman hits Macon Jr., Hagar's refusals dwindle and she becomes unquestionably his, waiting for him when he is away and chiding him for not paying enough attention to her. While Milkman enjoys his sexual relationship with Hagar, he treats her like a "third beer," partaking of her because she is "there," rather than because he genuinely wants to pursue her. Never considering Hagar a girlfriend or future wife because of her lower social class, Milkman instead searches for a bride among the wealthy black women of Honoré, but finds them too boring for his taste. At age thirty-one he tires of Hagar and writes her a letter breaking off their relationship. Hagar is driven insane by the letter and rushes out to find Milkman.

Meanwhile, Milkman and Guitar have grown apart. Though they are still buddies, Milkman suspects that Guitar is concealing something from him. Guitar, in turn, chides Milkman for leading a careless, frivolous life. During one of their conversations, Milkman tells Guitar about a dream in which he sees his mother planting flower bulbs in their backyard. The flower bulbs, Milkman says, grow instantaneously, almost choking his mother. Although Milkman says that the vision was a dream, he knows that it was reality.

Unaware that Hagar is roaming the town's streets searching for him, Milkman chats with Freddie the janitor. Freddie tells Milkman that he believes in ghosts, and that his own mother went into labor, gave birth to him, and died after seeing a ghost of a white bull. Milkman shrugs with a smile. Freddie then tells Milkman about growing up in jail because Jacksonville, Florida, did not have facilities for black orphans. He also suggests that Guitar is involved in shady activities, including the recent murder of a white boy in their town.

ANALYSIS

Milkman is disconnected from his true identity in part because he rejects the love that he is given instead of returning it. For instance, just as the biblical Abraham banishes the handmaiden Hagar instead of marrying her after she bears him a child, so does Milkman discard Pilate's granddaughter Hagar when he no longer finds her useful. The fact that Milkman appreciates Hagar only for her physical attributes, without understanding her deep feelings toward him or ever reciprocating her respect, is symptomatic of his emotional shallowness. Only when Milkman eventually recovers his lost identity does he learn how to love those who love him.

Morrison's narrative often conveys Milkman's inner struggle by employing techniques of magical realism, a narrative form in which magical events occur as part of everyday life. Although the novel is situated within a real historical time frame (the historical Emmett Till was murdered in 1953), supernatural events are pervasive and generally accepted as normal by the characters. Morrison even uses magical realism to show the racial problems of mid–twentieth-century America in physical terms. For example, the ghostly white bull that terrifies Freddie's mother and whose appearance seems to speed Freddie's birth is a striking symbol of overwhelming white power and oppression. Similarly, the oppression to which Ruth is subject is also embodied in a supernatural event: her weak-minded submission to domestic terror is symbolized by the passive welcome she extends to monstrous flower bulbs that try to choke her. The aggressive, magical realist aspect of these supernatural encounters makes racism and sexism all the more immediate to us.

Though all of the novel's characters witness supernatural events, only Milkman is unwilling to acknowledge their existence publicly. Even though he sees the flowers choking his mother, when he tells the story to Guitar he purposefully claims it was a dream in order to avoid seeming like a fool who believes in fairly tales. Furthermore, though Milkman is not bold enough in his conversation with Freddie to deny the existence of ghosts outright, his smirking disdain for the janitor's story suggests that he considers belief in the supernatural to be a mark of either stupidity or low social standing. In short, Milkman rejects the paranormal because he is concerned about his self-image and about being seen by others as a strange freak. But because the supernatural is part of the reality of *Song of Solomon*'s world, Milkman's failure to accept the supernatural actually makes him abnormal.

CHAPTER 5

SUMMARY

Driven mad by her overpowering love, Hagar ceases to be interested in anything other than Milkman. She obsesses over being abandonded, and remains depressed despite Pilate and Reba's attempts to comfort her. Milkman spends much of his time at Guitar's place, hiding from Hagar, who roams the streets of their town and periodically tries to kill him. Meanwhile, Guitar has become paranoid and politically active, triple-locking his doors at night and lecturing to Milkman about the oppression of African-Americans and other subjugated peoples around the world. One night, as Guitar continues to chide Milkman about being wealthy and well-dressed, Milkman confronts him, asking him to account for his secret activities. Guitar only smiles in response, and leaves for a mysterious house where six old men wait for him. Milkman remains alone in the Southside flat on a night when both expect Hagar to make another attempt to murder him.

As Milkman lies alone in Guitar's bed, he remembers how he came to discover one of his mother's darkest secrets only a week before. Milkman recalls how he witnessed his mother leaving Not Doctor Street on a bus late at night. Unbeknownst to Ruth, Milkman followed her to the county train station and then to Fairfield Cemetery, where Dr. Foster had been buried more than forty years earlier. Milkman waited for several hours outside the gates while Ruth was inside the cemetery and confronted her when she finally exited. On the ride back to town, Ruth gave Milkman an explanation of her relationship with Dr. Foster, one that challenged Macon Jr.'s version of the events. She told Milkman that she cherished her father because he was the only person in the world who cared about how she lived.

Milkman also recalls that Ruth told him that Macon Jr. had killed Dr. Foster by throwing away his medication and that their sex life had ended after Dr. Foster's death. Hungry for her husband's physical attention, Ruth had secretly fed him an aphrodisiac concocted by Pilate. Macon Jr. made love to Ruth for four days and Milkman was conceived.

Macon Jr. had tried to force Ruth to abort the baby. Pilate prevented the abortion by frightening Macon Jr. with a voodoo doll. Ruth acknowledged that she breast-fed Milkman past infancy and also claimed that she prayed for him every day and night.

Milkman stops ruminating when he hears Hagar's footsteps in the room. She enters with a butcher knife. Instead of getting up and stopping her, Milkman closes his eyes and wills her dead. He asks an unseen power to choose between him and her. She strikes him on the collarbone with the knife, but the blow is harmless, and she is unable to make another attempt. Milkman sits up, throws Hagar a few jeering remarks, and turns away.

Within a short time, Ruth finds out about Hagar's murderous behavior and goes to see Pilate. Because she has always seen Milkman as her "passion" and her "single triumph," rather than a separate person, Ruth is determined to keep him out of harm's way. On the porch of Pilate's home, Ruth threatens Hagar. Ruth and Hagar heatedly discuss their love for Milkman until Pilate interrupts and tells them that it is silly for a woman to feel so much for any man. Pilate then tells Ruth the story of her childhood. She had worked diligently as a migrant worker but was driven out of each place because people were terrified of a woman with no navel. Pilate settled down on a Virginia island for a few years, and found a good man who fathered Reba. Despite being in love, she refused to marry him. After Reba gave birth to Hagar, Pilate moved her family to Macon Jr.'s town, bringing a green sack from Lincoln's Heaven as one of her few possessions. The ghost of Macon Dead I, Pilate claims, followed her, sometimes speaking to her and murmuring the word "sing." Pilate also tells Ruth that she became a wine-maker and seller because it was the job that afforded her the most independence. Finally, Pilate concludes her story, which she has deliberately made long to keep Ruth's mind off Hagar.

ANALYSIS

Song of Solomon takes place within a political context, and the characters of Guitar and Milkman represent different attitudes toward the civil rights of African-Americans. Guitar is a radical revolutionary, whose views are a combination of those put forth by Elijah Mohammed and Malcom X, leaders of Islamic religious groups that fought for black self-sufficiency and separation from whites. Guitar's involvement, we later learn, with the anti-white Seven Days group makes him an extremist within the radical community. Milkman represents the calmness of the Northern black upper-middle class, which did little while blacks in the South were beaten and imprisoned. Morrison does not give us a character who embodies the principles of nonviolent resistance put forth by Martin Luther King, Jr., the leader of the 1960s civil rights movement. Instead, Morrison purposefully presents only the extreme viewpoints embodied by Milkman and Guitar to heighten their eventual clash.

The novel idealizes strong women, painting in an unfavorable light those female characters who depend on men for survival. While Ruth and Hagar are from different classes, generations, and social groups, each harbors a love for Milkman that stifles her personal development. After Milkman abandons her, Hagar can do nothing but think about her former lover. Although Hagar's love may seem selfless, it is actually consumingly selfish, as she needs Milkman to survive. Ruth, who cannot bear the thought of harm coming to her boy, is also unwittingly motivated by selfishness, viewing Milkman as a triumph over her husband's despotism. Although Ruth suffers under Macon Jr.'s wrath for many years, she does not leave him, nor does she directly stand up to him. Rather, she continues to draw on his money to maintain her upper-class lifestyle just as Hagar tries to lure Milkman's affection for her own needs. Both women are not only powerless before and completely dependent upon men, but also self-serving.

In contrast to the weak Hagar and Ruth, Morrison elevates Pilate to the status of an admirable female role model. She is the only woman in the novel who does not define herself according to the love a man holds for her. She does not need anyone's affirmation. Surviving by her own means and wits, Pilate radiates strength. She is named after Pontius Pilate, the Roman politician who, according to the New Testament, presided over Jesus' crucifixion. Like her namesake, Morrison's Pilate is a powerful figure, but unlike him she is completely free of evil. Nevertheless, Morrison reminds us that women who are self-assured and independent are actually feared, shunned, and treated as though they are evil. Pilate must pay the price of alienation for her freedom.

In this part of the novel Morrison uses supernatural situations and events to examine Pilate's and Milkman's independence and power over others. Morrison symbolizes their strength and the alienation that comes with it through supernatural physical abnormalities: Milkman's leg shrinks and Pilate lacks a navel. Morrison also endows both characters with uncanny willpower over others. Pilate is able to fend off her brother's attacks on his wife and strike mortal fear into him with a simple rag doll. Similarly, Milkman is able not only to avert Hagar's knife from his throat by thought alone but also to will her eventual death and his own survival. These supernatural traits distinguish Milkman and Pilate from the other characters and heighten the importance of their respective journeys.

The narrative voice also gains importance in this section of *Song of Solomon*. Much of the novel develops through dialogue in which the narrator's voice is almost entirely absent. However, the narrator's interjections are essential to the plot. We learn about certain events from a series of competing narratives: Macon Jr. and Ruth, for example, give Milkman contradictory explanations of Dr. Foster's relationship with Ruth. In this case, the narrator brings us a more accurate account than either character, telling us in the first chapter that Dr. Foster notices Ruth's inappropriate affection for him and is secretly glad when she marries. Thus, while Milkman has only his father's and mother's takes on the relationship from which to draw a conclusion, we, as readers, have the additional advantage of being able to hear Dr. Foster's point of view and thus evaluate the matter more objectively.

CHAPTERS 6–7

SUMMARY: CHAPTER 6

Milkman confronts Guitar and asks him to reveal the reasons for his secretive behavior. Guitar tells him that he belongs to a secret society called the Seven Days. The organization, composed of seven black men each of whom is assigned a day of the week, kill white people at random every time that a black person is murdered and the assailants are left unpunished. Guitar says that Robert Smith and Henry Porter were both members. The Seven Days try to make each revenge killing similar to the original violence against the black victim. If he was hanged, for example, they hang their next victim. These revenge killings are performed on the same day of the week as the original murders of the black victims. Guitar is the only young man in the group.

Guitar tells Milkman that his activities are driven by the firm belief that whites are "unnatural" people who would murder and pillage in the right circumstances. The twentieth-century German leader Adolf Hitler, Guitar argues, murdered Jews because there were no blacks around. Furthermore, he continues, blacks need to take drastic measures to avenge assaults against them. Unlike Jews who survived World War II concentration camps, they do not have recourse to legal action. Guitar concludes by saying that his actions help keep the ratio of blacks to whites balanced, ensuring that whites will not gain an upper hand by means of genocide.

Milkman counters Guitar's rhetoric by telling him that many whites have made real sacrifices on behalf of African-Americans. He also asks why Guitar does not change his name, like Malcom X did, in order to show that he refuses to accept his "slave name." But Guitar answers that his slave name, Bains, does not bother him—only his slave status does. To no avail, Milkman begs Guitar to see him and others as human beings rather than whites or blacks. Milkman finishes his conversation with Guitar by telling him that Guitar's murderous activities are "crazy," that they have become a "habit," and that since he is able to kill so callously, he might move toward killing black people, including Milkman himself.

SUMMARY: CHAPTER 7

> *Life, safety, and luxury fanned out before him like the*
> *tailspread of a peacock.*   (See QUOTATIONS, p. 58)

After his conversation with Guitar, Milkman goes to speak with Macon Jr. Stifled from spending over thirty years at home, he asks Macon Jr. if he can leave home for a year to travel and explore his personal interests. During the conversation, Milkman unintentionally mentions the green sack hanging from Pilate's ceiling.

Macon Jr. interrupts Milkman and his eyes begin to gleam. He tells Milkman about the days after his father's murder. For two weeks, Macon Jr. and Pilate hid in a manor house where Circe, the midwife, worked as a maid. While in hiding, Pilate put a brown piece of paper with her name on it in a snuffbox, attached a wire to the box, and began to wear it as an earring. After Macon and Pilate left Circe, they traveled across the countryside, encountered their father's ghost sitting on a tree trunk, and then saw the ghost again at the mouth of a cave. The siblings followed the ghost into the cave and spent the night there. In the morning, Macon Jr. became aware that there was someone else in the cave: an old, white man. Terrified that he was seeing an apparition, Macon Jr. killed the man. Underneath the man's green tarp, Macon Jr. discovered a treasure of gold nuggets. Macon Jr. imagined a life of luxury spread out before him "like the tailspread of a peacock," but then they saw their father standing before them. Macon Dead I then disappeared and Pilate darted around the cave looking for him. Macon Jr. wanted to take the treasure, but Pilate urged him not to. They fought. Macon Jr. left and came back three days later, finding the dead man still there, but Pilate, the tarpaulin, and the gold were gone.

After hearing Milkman mention the green tarpaulin, Macon Jr. becomes convinced that it is full of the dead man's treasure. He urges his son to "get the gold" so that they can share it.

ANALYSIS: CHAPTERS 6–7

Guitar's anger is justified and his love for African-Americans admirable, but the manner in which he expresses his love—murder—is disgraceful and pointless. Traumatized by the childhood death of his father, Guitar moves from being a sensitive young man to a heartless killer. Because murdering others grows to be a habit, Guitar gains the same "unnatural" qualities that he accuses whites of having. Just like whites, whom he accuses of being ready to murder anyone if the right conditions exist, Guitar is on his way to becoming a reckless killer. Milkman's question as to whether or not Guitar could kill a black person like Milkman ultimately proves prophetic. Although Guitar claims that his deeds are grounded in a clear philosophy, his distinction between murdering out of love for black people and murdering out of hate for white people is blurry. Through his question, Milkman points out that loving a group of people because of the color of their skin is also a form of racism because it involves rejecting a particular person as an individual and treating him or her solely as a member of a group.

That Guitar is the only young member of the Seven Days suggests that his beliefs—those he expresses to Milkman—are outdated. His hidden, terrorist way of thinking and operating is no longer justifiable or necessary in the burgeoning civil rights climate of the 1960s. During this era, African-Americans gained access to new ways of dealing with racism, ranging from Martin Luther King, Jr.'s policy of peaceful protest to Malcolm X's policy of open agitation. Whereas such leaders and their followers were able to channel their anger about racial oppression into a socially productive course of action, the immature Guitar lets his anger explode into acts of revenge, with no thought for the consequences.

Milkman's demand that Guitar see him as a human being rather than just a black man, however, may be too idealistic at a time when African-Americans were persecuted for the color of their skin. When we consider Milkman's comments alongside his careless lifestyle, they begin to sound slightly hollow. Furthermore, Milkman seems to be more concerned with his "slave name"—Macon Dead III—than his "slave status"—the possibility of facing discrimination because of his race. But, even though Guitar suggests that Milkman is concerned with the wrong issues, the novel's emphasis on one's name as an important part of one's identity illustrates that one's slave name is an undeniable part of one's slave status. Only by rediscovering their true names, which lie beneath their slave names, can the characters free themselves from oppression.

The shift from the first-person narrative to the third-person in the story about the gold forces us to question whether or not the narrator is reliable. Because events of the past in the novel have usually been recounted to us by a character, this interruption by the narrator is abnormal and should make us wary. Unlike the conflicting stories that Macon Jr. and Ruth tell Milkman about their life and relationship prior to his birth, the story of the gold in the cave is not quoted from one of the characters—we receive only the narrator's version of events. Morrison's decision to allow the narrator to speak to us directly here compels us to question whether the narrator, like the individual characters, has a particular motive in telling the story. We must question whether he or she is trying to persuade us to see the story from a particular point of view so that we see the characters in a particular light, either favorable or unfavorable.

Chapters 8–9

Summary: Chapter 8

Guitar lies in his bed, figuring out how to bomb a white church and kill four little white girls in order to avenge the Birmingham church bombing, in which four little black girls perished. Guitar's plans hit a dead end because he does not have enough money to purchase explosives. Milkman then arrives and tells Guitar about the treasure Pilate is supposedly hoarding in the green tarp. The two friends fantasize about how to get the loot, devise ways to get it out of Pilate's house, and relish all the possibilities the money will bring.

During Milkman and Guitar's conversation, a mysterious white peacock leaps off a building and struts around the street in front of them. Guitar and Milkman attempt to catch the peacock, but then lose themselves in fantasies about the gold. Guitar briefly thinks that he could use the money to help out his grandmother and siblings but then recalls that he needs the money for his Seven Days mission.

Meanwhile, Milkman realizes that having a large sum of money would liberate him by making him independent from his father. The following night, Guitar and Milkman steal into Pilate's house and cut down the green bundle. On their way out, Guitar thinks he sees a figure of a man standing right behind Milkman. As the pair leaves Pilate's place, Reba, who is awake, wonders what the robbers might want with the bundle.

SUMMARY: CHAPTER 9

The narrator tells us that First Corinthians is secretly working as a maid for Michael-Mary Graham, the state poet laureate. Although First Corinthians graduated from Bryn Mawr and has been to France, no man of her social class is interested in marrying her because she is too "accustomed to middle-class life." Though her parents think she is working as Graham's secretary, First Corinthians has taken the job as a maid in order to get out of Macon Jr.'s house and feel independent.

On her bus rides home from work, First Corinthians is courted by an elderly black man, who we later learn is Henry Porter. Porter works as a yardman and is a Southside tenant of Macon Jr.'s, and he and First Corinthians begin to date in secret. He eventually confronts her and asks her if she is ashamed to be dating him. First Corinthians says that she is not. But after she realizes that she is in love with Porter and that he might leave her forever because she is not a "doll-baby," she admits that she has not been fair to Porter. They go to his place and make love.

When First Corinthians returns home to Not Doctor Street, she overhears a loud argument between Macon Jr. and Milkman. During the argument it comes out that while driving with the tarp bundle in their car after the robbery, Guitar and Milkman were pulled over by a cop, searched, and taken to the police station. The bundle, as it turns out, is not filled with gold but with rocks and a human skeleton. Both Macon Jr. and Pilate come to the station to bail them out. Pilate plays the act of an ignorant old woman, and tells a story about how the bones belonged to her dead husband, Mr. Solomon. The cops believe Pilate's story, return the bundle to her, and let the two men go. Milkman recalls that on the ride back from the station, Pilate told Macon Jr. that she never took the gold, but instead came back to the cave three years after she and Macon Jr. parted to collect the bones of the dead white man. Pilate claimed that Macon Dead I ordered her to come back because she could not "fly on off and leave a body."

While they are sitting in the den of their house in the middle of the night, Macon Jr. yells at Milkman, asking him why he took along Guitar, "that Southside nigger." Milkman refuses to respond to his father's provocations and is instead shocked by the fact that the cops stopped him without a good reason. Milkman calls his father crazy, but Macon Jr. says that if Pilate did not take the gold then it must still be in the cave, and that someone should retrieve it.

Milkman goes to sleep and wakes up at noon. He stands in front of the mirror in his bathroom and feels a profound sense of shame over stealing the green tarp. While reviewing the events of the previous day, Milkman realizes that Guitar has killed before and is capable of killing again. As he gazes into the mirror, Milkman notices that his undersized leg seems to have returned to normal length.

Milkman then walks outside, sees an old Oldsmobile packed with Guitar and six other friends, Porter among them, and realizes that Porter, a member of the Seven Days, is the man First Corinthians is secretly seeing. After Milkman informs Macon Jr. of his discovery, Macon Jr. breaks up the relationship, evicts Porter from his dwelling, and forces First Corinthians to quit her job.

A few days later, Lena confronts Milkman and harshly rebukes him for ending First Corinthians's only relationship. She tells Milkman that he is just like Macon Jr., living off Ruth's, First Corinthians's, and her own labor without doing anything himself. Lena reminds Milkman of the time when he, then just a little boy, urinated on her. She claims that in one way or another, Milkman has been urinating on others his entire life, and that he is a "sad, pitiful, stupid, selfish, hateful man" without anything to show for himself except the "little hog's gut" that hangs between his legs. Lena ends her rebuke by telling Milkman that she will no longer make artificial roses and sends Milkman away from her room.

ANALYSIS: CHAPTERS 8–9

Throughout the novel, white creatures are symbols of impending harm or wrongdoing. In this section, the white peacock seen by Guitar and Milkman, like the white bull that caused the labor and subsequent death of Freddie's mother, is a phantom of evil. The two men's pursuit of the white peacock symbolizes their greed. The peacock itself symbolizes the corrupting allure of wealth, just as when Macon Jr. saw the gold in the cave as a spread peacock's tail and became obsessed with accumulating wealth. This greed is evil because it makes Macon Jr. a tyrant and eventually turns Guitar against Milkman. That these apparitions are specifically white evokes the idea of white oppression of blacks: the white bull effectively renders Freddie an orphan and forces him to grow up in jail because there are no facilities for black orphans, while the white peacock appeals to Guitar's sense of blacks being the victims of economic injustice.

Milkman's emotions following the theft of the tarp reflect his ongoing, intensifying transformation from a "Dead" man into a living one. The shame Milkman feels after robbing Pilate serves as evidence of his spiritual awakening. It is no coincidence that while he experiences this shame his undersized leg—the physical abnormality that represents his emotional childishness—appears perfectly normal again. The lame leg that seems miraculously cured demonstrates that Milkman's shame is the beginning of a deeper transformation. Now that he is able to understand his actions and his way of life objectively and to see the immaturity of his lifestyle, he can repair his flaws and become a better person.

Milkman's experience of being pulled over by a white cop without probable cause, or good reason, marks the end of his privileged, idealistic worldview. This incident proves to Milkman that, in the eyes of the law, he is just another black man, guilty before proven innocent. Ironically, the dehumanizing police station experience that follows Milkman's arrest gives him a taste of being a part of the greater African-American community, from which he has always been alienated. Entering this community endows Milkman with compassion. In fact, we know that he tells Macon Jr. about Porter's relationship with First Corinthians because he is genuinely concerned about her welfare, rather than—as Lena suggests—because Porter is of a lower social class. Lena viciously rebukes Milkman, equating his tyranny with Macon Jr.'s, because she does not realize that the Milkman before her is evolving from a selfish person into a caring one.

Milkman is not the only character who undergoes a transformation. His sisters, First Corinthians and Lena, whom Morrison keeps in the background of the novel's main events, are suddenly transformed into deep, complex characters. The two sisters, who have spent their lives in Dr. Foster's parlor making artificial roses, which are symbols of fake love, refuse to be aristocratic sweatshop workers any longer. The fact that First Corinthians works as a maid despite her college degree does not demean her but rather liberates her economically and socially. Furthermore, the fact that she finds true love only outside the strict confines of her class shows that Morrison is making an attack on class-consciousness in general. Lena's revolt comes out during her confrontation with Milkman. Even though she may be mistaken about the nature of Milkman's now-transformed character, her rebuke is fully justifiable and represents the revolt of the novel's repressed female characters. Lena speaks not only for herself, but also for her mother, sister, and every other abused, subjugated, or abandoned woman in the novel.

The confusion about the location of the gold illustrates the difficult nature of Milkman's journey toward self-discovery. When Macon Jr. prepares to tell Milkman his story after Milkman first mentions the tarp at Pilate's house, the narrator cuts in to tell us that the gold was not in the cave when Macon Jr. came back three days after murdering the old white man. But Macon Jr.'s suggestion to Milkman that the gold may still be inside the cave conflicts with the narrator's version of the story. Because Milkman does not have our luxury of sifting through conflicting narratives, he can follow only the erroneous roadmap that Macon Jr. lays out for him. This wasted effort teaches Milkman a lesson: although he has spent his life idling, he must now work hard for his reward, the eventual recovery of his identity.

CHAPTER 10

SUMMARY

Milkman speaks to Guitar and tells him that he intends to go to Montour County, Pennsylvania, to look for the gold in the cave. He says that he will go alone but that he will split any treasure he finds with Guitar. Guitar suspects that Milkman might cheat him. He reminds Milkman that he needs the money to carry out his Seven Days mission and to help support Henry Porter, who has been evicted in the aftermath of his affair with First Corinthians. Their conversation ends on a sour note.

Milkman takes a plane to Pittsburgh, relishing the flight, and then takes a bus to Danville, Pennsylvania, the town nearest Lincoln's Heaven. In Danville, he finds an old friend of his father's, Reverend Cooper, who tells Milkman that he knows his "people." As Reverend Cooper tells Milkman stories about his father's boyhood, Macon Dead I, and Circe, Milkman feels a warm glow. He realizes that Macon Jr. had a close relationship with Macon Dead I and loved him. Reverend Cooper also tells Milkman that the Butlers, the wealthy white family that employed Circe, were responsible for Macon Dead I's murder.

Milkman makes his way toward Lincoln's Heaven, and stops by the now run-down Butler mansion on the way. He walks inside and is startled by a rotting stench that quickly turns into a pleasant ginger scent. He sees a spiraling staircase and remembers seeing such a staircase in his childhood dreams. An ancient woman, "colorless" with age, stands at the top of the staircase and hugs Milkman. She confirms that she is Circe, his father's midwife. At first, Circe mistakes Milkman for Macon Jr., and is disappointed when she discovers that she is looking at the wrong Macon Dead.

Circe tells Milkman that Macon Dead I's real name was Jake, that his wife's name was Sing, and that they came to Pennsylvania in a wagon from a place in Virginia called Charlemagne. Circe adds that the deceased owners of the mansion, the Butlers, earned their wealth by robbing and killing poor, independent farmers such as Macon Dead I. She also reveals that a month after his burial, the murdered Macon Dead I's body floated out of its grave during the first rain and was deposited by hunters in the same cave where Macon Jr. and Pilate stayed. Under the pretense of wanting to find and bury his grandfather's bones, Milkman procures directions to the cave (called Hunter's Cave) from Circe. He offers to help Circe leave the Butlers' rotting mansion, which she occupies alone with a pack of weimaraner dogs. But Circe is determined to stay in the house of her hated masters because she wants to make sure it rots to the ground.

Macon leaves the Butler mansion and trudges through the thicket toward Hunter's Cave, ruining his expensive suit and shoes, and damaging his gold watch. He is driven by an unquenchable desire to find the gold. When Milkman reaches the cave, all he finds inside are some boards and a tin cup.

Milkman goes back to the highway and hitchhikes to the Danville bus station with a man named Fred Garnett. Milkman offers to pay the man for the ride, but Garnett does not take Milkman's money and drives away, offended. Milkman then goes inside the bus station's diner, where he helps a man load a huge crate onto a weighing platform. Milkman decides that Pilate must have taken the gold with her to Virginia and resolves to follow in her footsteps.

ANALYSIS

Milkman's journey, at first a greedy search for hidden treasure, becomes a meaningful quest for self-understanding. Although Milkman claims that gold is the ultimate goal of his journey, his motives for the gold are less convincing than his desire to seek out his family history. His reasoning behind going to Virginia to find Pilate's gold is illogical. There is no evidence to suggest that Pilate took the gold with her to Virginia or ever had it in her possession. While it could be argued that Milkman's desire for gold blinds him to better judgment, it is also possible that Milkman is purposefully trying to come up with a selfish reason to visit Virginia, because he cannot yet admit to himself that he is becoming a new man and that his journey south is not motivated by greed.

In stepping out of his self-absorbtion Milkman finds the path to personal fulfillment and independence from his father. At the Danville bus station, for instance, Milkman does something that seems out of character. Whereas earlier, he humors Hagar and her love only for sexual satisfaction, he now selflessly helps a man lift a crate. Furthermore, when his greedy tendencies arise, they actually set Milkman apart from his father. Greed is an end in itself for Macon Jr.: he is driven solely by the desire to accumulate profit. For Milkman, on the other hand, the gold offers the opportunity to escape the confines of privileged life. He wants it because it would give him the freedom to break out of his father's oppressive environment and allow him to find his own road in life.

As Milkman's quest progresses, the mythical world and the world of reality blend together. Circe, uncannily similar to the imaginary witch of Milkman's childhood dreams, appears to him to be so wispy that he is unsure whether she is a mirage or a living person. Milkman leaves Circe convinced that she is a living, though ancient, woman, but her airy, disheveled appearance, young woman's voice, and ability to transform a stench of decay into a pleasant fragrance make us think that she must be some sort of supernatural figure, after all. Ultimately, Milkman's encounter with Circe situates his own quest within Circe's mythic description of Macon Jr.'s and Pilate's early years. Just as Milkman is unsure whether Circe is a living woman or a ghost, we wonder whether Milkman's newly recovered past is historically accurate or simply part of an old folk tale.

The decay of the Butlers' mansion and the disintegration of the Butler family represent the collapse of the old sharecropping order and values. Just as the manor crumbles into disrepair, so did the Butlers fall from grace—dying alone and forgotten after leading a life of luxury, their memory cursed by their neighbors. That their possessions were devoured by their own dogs is the ultimate humiliation, as though their family trappings were nothing more than worthless scraps. The Butler mansion also symbolizes the emptiness of possessing material goods. Like Macon Jr., the Butlers dedicated their life to money, losing their humanity in the process. After losing their ill-gotten wealth, the Butlers were unable to go on living. They died not because they lacked food or clothing, but because they lacked money, the only good that nourished them.

Part II of Morrison's novel is inspired by Homer's ancient Greek epic the *Odyssey.* Much like the *Odyssey,* in which Odysseus makes his way home after twenty years of warring and traveling, Part II of *Song of Solomon* describes the hero's quest to come home. As we learn, even though Milkman was born and grew up in Michigan, his home lies elsewhere—in Pennsylvania and Virginia. Nevertheless, Milkman's journey follows Odysseus's and at times Morrison alerts us to this parallel with obvious references. In Homer's epic, Circe is the enchantress who keeps Odysseus on her island for a year but then helps him on his journey home. Likewise, in Morrison's novel, Circe points Milkman to Macon Dead I's birthplace and tells him his grandparents' original names, thus helping Milkman reach his ancestral home. Critic Sandra Adell gives an alternative explanation of Circe's role in *Song of Solomon.* She offers that Circe is also the ancient Greek goddess of the *omphalos,* or navel. Consequently, argues Adell, Circe acts out her mythical role, her help serving as an umbilical cord that reconnects Milkman with a forgotten past.

CHAPTER 11

SUMMARY

Milkman buys a cheap car and reaches Shalimar, his ancestral home in Virginia, where his car breaks down next to Solomon's General Store. Walking past women who remind him of Pilate, Milkman enters the store and is told by its proprietor, Mr. Solomon, that an unnamed friend of his drove by earlier, leaving a message that "your day is here."

Milkman realizes that the man was Guitar, and wonders why Guitar's message contained the executioner's call of the Seven Days. Milkman goes outside Solomon's store, and sees children playing a game and singing a song about Jay, the only son of someone named Solomon. Seeing the children evokes in Milkman memories of his own dreary childhood, which was marred by grieving over his inability to fly. When Milkman goes back inside the store, he finds himself burned by hostile stares from local men. After a few heated words, Milkman ends up in a fight with one of them, who is named Saul. While defending himself with a broken bottle, Milkman is cut with a knife on his face and left hand.

Older men in Solomon's Store compliment Milkman's bottle-swinging prowess and invite him to join them on a hunting trip. Though Milkman has never held a rifle in his life, he responds with bravado and agrees to come along. The men—Calvin, Luther Solomon, Omar, King Walker, Vernell, and Small Boy—strip Milkman of his suit, dress him in military fatigues, and hand him a Winchester rifle. The hunting party reaches its destination, Ryna's Gulch, late at night. The wind echoes in Ryna's Gulch eerily and local legend claims that the sounds come from a woman crying in the ravine. As the other men plan out the details of the hunt, Milkman notices a strange car speed past them.

The hunters divide into pairs, Milkman partnered with Calvin. They trek through the woods stalking a bobcat for several hours until Milkman becomes exhausted and stops to rest, leaving Calvin to continue the hunt alone. Lying in the dark under the Virginia sky, Milkman loses himself in thought. He comes to understand that he has always taken his privileged status for granted, that he has mistreated people who have loved him, such as Hagar, all the while indulging in self-pity. Away from his wealth and distinguished parentage, Milkman is forced to evaluate himself honestly and to see what he is actually capable of on his own.

Milkman's ruminations are interrupted when Guitar appears behind him and starts choking him with a wire, repeating again the Seven Days' trademark phrase, "your day has come." Milkman sees colored lights and hears music. His life flashes before him, but it consists of only one image—that of Hagar bending over him "in perfect love, in the most intimate sexual gesture imaginable." Milkman relaxes, surrendering to Guitar's murderous hands and breathes what he thinks is his last breath. Suddenly feeling invigorated, he manages to fire his Winchester rifle and scare Guitar off just as the men from the hunting party return, with a bobcat as their prize. The hunters, unaware of the recent attempt on Milkman's life, make fun of him for accidentally firing the rifle. Unaffected by their comments, Milkman walks on the earth "like he belong[s] on it," for the first time not limping.

The following day, over breakfast, Milkman finds out that his grandmother, Sing, was an Indian, the daughter of a woman named Heddy. Another of Heddy's descendants, Susan Byrd, lives in the area and Milkman decides to visit her. Before heading to Susan's, however, Milkman spends the night with a local prostitute, a beautiful woman whose personality is echoed in her name, Sweet. Sweet bathes Milkman and makes love to him, bringing him much pleasure in the process. In return, Milkman bathes Sweet, makes her bed, and scours her tub, while she makes him gumbo, puts salve on his neck, and launders his clothing. After giving Sweet fifty dollars, Milkman leaves, saying that he will see her that night.

ANALYSIS

Chapter 11 is written as a bildungsroman, a story that describes the maturation of a young hero into an adult. Finding himself in a completely unfamiliar place where his urban life experience is a handicap, where his father's wealth cannot shield him from harm, where locals (like Saul) tend to dislike him rather than adore him, Milkman is quickly forced to evaluate his life. Under the dark Virginia sky, Milkman dispenses with the self-praise and self-pity that characterize his privileged childhood. He begins to judge himself fairly, finally becoming able to admit his own wrongdoings. Milkman's changing out of his nice suit and into military clothes signifies his transformation from a child into an adult. He has outgrown both the literal wardrobe of his fancy clothes and the metaphorical wardrobe of his sheltered upbringing.

The spiritual and metaphorical transformation that Milkman experiences goes hand in hand with his physical rebirth from the jaws of death during Guitar's attack on him. Guitar's attack forces Milkman not only to face death but actually to experience it. The wording of the text in the attack scene suggests that Milkman dies and is instantly resurrected: "[h]e . . . saw a burst of many-colored lights dancing before his eyes. . . . When the music followed the colored lights, he knew he had just drawn the last sweet air left for him in the world." The wordplay spell cast over the novel—that Milkman cannot be killed because he is already "Dead"—is finally broken. One can argue that Milkman is killed by his way of living before a new way of living resurrects him. That is, Guitar's murder attempt comes at a moment when Milkman is finally casting off the deadness that has characterized him throughout the novel, when he is beginning to experience selfless compassion toward others.

Following his resurrection, Milkman is no longer the outsider he has been his whole life. He now belongs to a human community and *feels* that he belongs to it. Milkman's laughter with the hunters after surviving his assassination is evidence of his rebirth into a life of interacting meaningfully with others. Whereas earlier he feels fake compassion and fake understanding of racism, he now feels and expresses true emotions. The disappearance of the physical manifestations of Milkman's deadness—the undersized leg and the limp that accompanies it—show that he has been cured of his alienation.

We see evidence of Milkman's new identity in his positive interaction with Sweet. Unlike his relationship with Hagar, in which he uses her for sex but never returns her overwhelming love, Milkman engages in a mutually fulfilling relationship with Sweet. He bathes her after she bathes him; he gives her a back massage and she salves his wounds; he cleans her bathroom and she feeds him. It is no accident that Hagar "bending over him in perfect love" is the prevalent image that Milkman sees while Guitar tries to kill him. This image symbolizes both the degree of Hagar's generosity and also the extent of Milkman's mistreatment of her. In his extraordinarily respectful, fair-minded behavior toward Sweet, Milkman demonstrates that he has learned from his past mistakes and has matured.

CHAPTERS 12–13

SUMMARY: CHAPTER 12

> *Solomon cut across the sky, Solomon gone home.*
> (See QUOTATIONS, p. 59)

After spending the night with Sweet, Milkman visits Susan Byrd, simultaneously meeting a young woman named Grace Long, who seems smitten by him. It turns out that Susan Byrd's deceased father, Crowell, had a sister named Sing, but Susan claims that this Sing never married and left Virginia in a wagon headed for Massachusetts, not Pennsylvania. Disappointed that his clues seem to have led him to a dead end, Milkman leaves dissatisfied, forgetting his watch, and taking with him only a box of cookies and Grace Long's address in the box.

Walking along the path from Susan's house, Milkman realizes that his family history means a great deal to him and that it is important to find "his own people." As he journeys back to Sweet's place, he encounters Guitar. Guitar accuses Milkman of stealing the gold from the cave and shipping it to Virginia. Although Milkman denies doing so, Guitar is convinced of Milkman's treachery, announcing that he saw Milkman helping an old man lift a heavy crate onto a weighing platform back in Danville. Having never seen Milkman perform a selfless act, Guitar finds Milkman's assisting of the old man suspicious. Believing that Milkman has stolen the gold, thereby preventing Guitar from carrying out his mission for the Seven Days, Guitar promises to do everything possible to kill him. When Milkman asks why Guitar left him a warning about his impending demise at Solomon's store, Guitar replies that it was the least he could do for a friend.

Following his conversation with Guitar, Milkman spends another night with Sweet, and then returns to Shalimar. The events of the few previous days make Milkman realize that he sorely misses Pilate. He also sees his parents' flaws and positive qualities in a more objective light, and understands that their life experience scarred them. Finally, Milkman regrets his treatment of Hagar and becomes aware that he thrived off her mad desire for him because it validated his manhood.

Taking a break from his thoughts, Milkman again hears the local children sing a song about Jay, the only son of Solomon. He memorizes the entire song, according to which Solomon flew home across the sky, leaving a woman named Ryna to cry for him, weeping that cotton balls will choke her. The song also relates that Jay was raised by a woman named Heddy in a "red man's house." As he listens, Milkman realizes that the song is about his grandfather, Macon Dead I, formerly known as Jake, and his great-grandfather, Solomon. He also understands that Susan Byrd did not tell him everything she knew. He resolves to visit her again, thrilled by his discovery.

SUMMARY: CHAPTER 13

Guitar returns to Michigan to find Hagar, despondent and nude, standing listlessly in his room. Feeling sorry for her, Guitar drives Hagar home, urging her along the way to stop destroying herself over Milkman. Pilate and Reba also try unsuccessfully to cheer up Hagar. Suddenly waking from her catatonic state, Hagar rushes into a flurry of activity, believing that if she only improves her physical appearance Milkman will grow to love her.

Reba pawns her Sears diamond for $200 and sends Hagar on a shopping spree. In a mad rush to make herself over, Hagar dashes from store to store, purchasing a variety of cosmetics and fashion garments: a garter belt, colorless pantyhose, panties, and nylon slips. On her way home, Hagar is caught in a torrential thunderstorm and her purchases are damaged. Nevertheless, she scurries into her bedroom, and, without drying herself, puts on her new getup. When she greets Pilate and Reba, she is a mess: her hose is "ripped," her white dress is "soiled," her face powder is "lumpy," and her hair is "wild." After a sudden commotion, Hagar collapses into a deep illness and soon dies.

Reba visits Macon Jr. at his office and he reluctantly gives Reba money for Hagar's funeral, a grand but sparsely attended affair. Near the conclusion of the ceremony, Pilate and Reba burst in, singing an old gospel tune, "Mercy." Pilate reaches the coffin and speaks to Hagar, repeatedly calling her "[m]y baby girl." Pilate concludes her lament by exclaiming, "And she was *loved!*"

ANALYSIS: CHAPTERS 12–13

The narrative's emphasis on the African-American oral tradition reflects Milkman's maturation. Historically, African slaves were prevented from becoming literate by their white masters, so they preserved their history and passed it on to future generations through songs and stories. Ultimately in *Song of Solomon,* Milkman's family history is conveyed by the spoken rather than the written word. Only by letting go of the traditional methods of historical research prevalent in the white world—searching through archives or registry records—and putting his faith in folk legends can Milkman uncover the truth about his family's origins. Milkman's ability to use this ancestral, oral tradition as a resource—being given clues by everyone from Macon Jr. to Circe to the singing children—attests to his transformation from a black man alienated from black culture into a black man who embraces black culture.

The act of learning the popular folk song about Solomon that the children teach one another reaffirms Milkman's status as a child in a new world. Spiritually reborn after surviving Guitar's assassination, Milkman must now, like a child, learn his way around. He is innocent, eager to learn, not spoiled and bored as he was during his actual childhood in Michigan. Most important, perhaps, he is aware of and curious about his heritage. The traditional folk song about Solomon introduces the children to their heritage, and by taking part in this formative experience, Milkman becomes one of them. That he feels so at home in this community illustrates the depth of his transformation.

Solomon's song expands upon two major ideas in the novel, flight and abandonment, and suggests that the destructive cycle that includes both of these is almost inescapable. Just as Solomon escaped slavery and left his wife, Ryna, to suffer alone in hot cotton fields, so does Milkman flee the confines of his dull existence in Michigan and leave Hagar to die of unrequited love. We can interpret this pattern of males abandoning females as a comment from Morrison on black social conditions. Slavery and continued subjugation by whites had a devastating effect on African-American families: the men were often absent, whether they were taken by force or left of their own accord, leaving women the burden of raising children alone. Many, like Guitar's mother, are unable to deal with their difficult task, scarring a new generation of children and perpetuating the same problems that have affected their generation. Morrison, however, does not blame the men or the women for their deeds. Rather, she shows that the social conditions that forced Solomon to fly away from the cotton fields and that force Milkman to run away from home are responsible for the continuing deprivation of the African-American community.

While Hagar's death can be traced to this cycle of flight and abandonment, Pilate and Reba are in continuous rebellion against this cycle. Although their best efforts to save Hagar's life prove inadequate, Pilate and Reba never cease to fight, even when Hagar is lying in a coffin. When Pilate lifts her head to the sky and shouts, "And she was *loved!*" she is not only grieving over her granddaughter but also expressing her dissatisfaction with a society, a world, and a God that would allow such a catastrophe. But Hagar loses her own struggle precisely because she does not believe that she is deserving of love. This belief is evident in her frantic attempts to improve herself physically. Though Reba and Pilate try to raise Hagar's confidence in her own natural appearance, Hagar thinks that she can break this cycle of flight and abandonment only by transforming herself into a physically attractive woman and luring Milkman back. However, the thunderstorm that opens on her after her shopping spree and her horrible appearance after putting on her damaged garments demonstrate the futility of her attempt to break the patterns of her heritage. Whereas Pilate and Reba are anchored to their identities and remain strong in the face of struggle, Hagar has become so self-hating that reminders of who she actually is—a thirty-seven-year-old, single, poor African-American woman—speed her death.

CHAPTERS 14–15

SUMMARY: CHAPTER 14
Milkman returns to Susan Byrd, who fills in the gaps in his new-found knowledge of his family history. Sing, it turns out, left on a wagon to go North with Jake, who belonged to the legendary tribe of flying African children, the descendants of Solomon. Solomon and his wife, Ryna, had been slaves on a cotton plantation and had had twenty-one children, all boys, the last one named Jake. When Solomon flew away from Virginia, he tried to take Jake, who was a baby at the time, with him. Unfortunately, Solomon brushed by some tree branches and dropped Jake, who fell from the sky into the yard of an Indian woman named Heddy. Heddy had a baby daughter named Singing Bird (later called Sing) and raised Jake as her own son after Ryna became insane following Solomon's flight. Eventually, Heddy had another son, Crow Bird (later called Crowell Byrd), who was to become Susan Byrd's father. Meanwhile, Jake and Sing secretly ran off together.

SUMMARY: CHAPTER 15
Milkman leaves Susan's home. He is profoundly energized by the information he receives from his newfound cousin. Exhilarated, he runs to Sweet's place and, refusing her offer of a bath, tells her he needs to swim in the "sea! The whole goddam sea!" Milkman and Sweet whirl around in the local swimming hole as Milkman sings Solomon's song at the top of his voice: "O-o-o-o-o-o Solomon done fly, Solomon done gone / Solomon cut across the sky, Solomon gone home!"

Eventually ready to return home to Michigan, Milkman sells his car and boards the bus, thinking along the way about his family in Michigan and in Virginia, about his recent journey, and about his broken friendship with Guitar. When he reaches his hometown, he rushes to Pilate's home to tell her about his discoveries, unaware of Hagar's recent death. Pilate knocks him out by striking him with a wine bottle on the head.

When Milkman wakes, he finds himself in Pilate's basement, surrounded by Hagar's things, and understands that she is dead. Milkman knows that Pilate lives by the idea that when one takes a life, one owns it, which is why she carries the green tarp containing what she thinks are the old white man's bones. Milkman understands that Pilate is trying to make him own Hagar's life and that he will have to carry this burden to the end of his days. When Pilate finally enters the basement, Milkman tells her that the bones in the green tarp are actually her father's, and that she must bury them. Pilate then releases Milkman, sending him home with a box of Hagar's hair.

At home, Milkman finds that First Corinthians has moved to a small house with Henry Porter on the Southside, that Lena, though unforgiving, has become civil, and that the relationship between Macon Jr. and Ruth remains as broken as ever. Nevertheless, Macon Jr. decides that he will eventually head down to Danville to see Reverend Cooper and some of the others.

Milkman and Pilate drive down to Virginia to bury Jake's bones. They reach Solomon's Leap, the cliff near which Solomon dropped Jake, and bury the contents of the green tarp. In place of a gravestone, Pilate leaves her snuff-box earring containing her name. Just as the burial rites are completed, Pilate collapses into Milkman's arms, shot by a bullet that Guitar intended for Milkman. Milkman comforts Pilate as much as he can, singing the last lines of Solomon's song to her, but replacing the name Solomon with Sugargirl. Despite his efforts, Pilate dies. A flock of birds appears over Milkman's head, two of which circle around him until one of them dives from the sky and retrieves the snuffbox from the grave.

After Pilate dies, Milkman stands up, unafraid of Guitar's gun. He calls out Guitar's name until he hears a response and sees Guitar's shadowy outline in the dark. Milkman leaps in his direction, knowing that "[i]f you surrendered to the air, you could *ride* it."

ANALYSIS: CHAPTERS 14–15

Understanding his family history allows Milkman to complete his rebirth. His earlier time in Virginia, singing Solomon's song and playing the games of local children, allows him to experience a childhood he never had, and the swim in the quarry hole with Sweet serves as his baptism into his new life. The most important aspect of this rebirth is Milkman's restored faith in flight, which redeems him culturally and spiritually. Though such a faith may seem irrelevant to Milkman's maturation, it echoes a common thread from the Afri-can-American Christian tradition: salvation through belief alone. Milkman's final utterance about riding on air illustrates his trust in the power of flight. Although Morrison ends the novel without tell-ing us what happens after Milkman leaps, this flight carries promise in it because it fulfills the failed promise of the novel's opening image, Robert Smith's leap off of Mercy Hospital.

The knowledge that Solomon did not bow humbly to being enslaved but instead liberated himself allows Milkman to break the generational cycle of trauma that has haunted him throughout his life. Flying, Milkman learns, does not have to be physical. Instead, Morrison's novel suggests, flying is the ability of a human being to overcome the obstacles in his or her path, to live a free life in a world that may be unfree. Pilate, for instance, has always been able to fly even though her feet never leave the ground and though she lives amid poverty, discrimination, and alienation. Furthermore, while most of the novel suggests that genetic traits, such as Milkman's lameness, prove debilitating, flight is explored as a positive genetic trait, suggesting that the generational history of African-Americans contains not only enslavement but also the necessary components for liberation.

Having undergone a rebirth and second childhood in Virginia, and having gained a purpose in his life, Milkman is now a responsi-ble adult. While he encourages Pilate to let go of the bones she has been carrying for years and to let her spirit rest, Milkman under-stands that he must pay his dues for causing Hagar's death. Just as Pilate carries what she believes are the old white man's bones because she considers herself guilty of taking his life, so will Milk-man carry the box of Hagar's hair that Pilate gives him. In his will-ingness to do so he not only expresses his respect for Hagar's deep love for him but also demonstrates ownership of her life. That is, he is now willing to acknowledge and take responsibility for his role in Hagar's death.

That Milkman cares not about the gold but about another trea-sure, the forgotten names of his ancestors, suggests that knowledge of one's family history is more important than any amount of mate-rial goods. Awareness of one's history, passed down through names, sustains the novel's characters more fruitfully than gold does. Though Milkman has finally learned this lesson, Pilate has known it all along. She carries her name in a snuff box in her ear because she knows it provides sustenance for her and can be a source of sustenance for future generations. Once she sees that Milkman knows and appreciates their ancestors' story, she no longer needs to carry the name physically, and places the snuffbox on Macon Dead I's new grave. Just as Pilate has carried around her name, an integral part of her identity, so now will Milkman carry around his story, an integral part of his identity.

Even in death, flight remains the symbol of life. The birds circling over Pilate's body after she is killed by Guitar's bullet suggest that physical death is not the end of her existence. The swooping down of one bird to take Pilate's snuffbox up to the sky indicates that her name will live on. And because she has so long clutched her name as a crucial part of her identity, it is clear that she too will live on. But even as Pilate's body lies still on the ground, Milkman himself takes flight. Having learned the story of his heritage he is now fully alive. We do not know whose death will result from Milkman's leap at Guitar, but Morrison suggests that whether Milkman kills or is killed doesn't really matter, since Milkman, now endowed with a rich sense of his identity, will live on after death just as Pilate will and just as Solomon has in the song that bears his name.

Important Quotations Explained

1. The singing woman . . . had wrapped herself up in an old quilt instead of a winter coat. Her head cocked to one side, her eyes fixed on Mr. Robert Smith, she sang in a powerful contralto.

This passage, from Chapter 1, describes Pilate's singing about Sugarman as Robert Smith prepares to fly off the roof of Mercy Hospital. In contrast to Ruth Foster, who wears expensive clothes, Pilate wears only an old quilt. Wearing the quilt shows that Pilate belongs to the community but is alienated from it. Pilate demonstrates her pride in her culture through the quilt, a traditional, homemade item in African-American households. Unlike Ruth, Pilate is proud of being a black woman and does not need to disguise herself in the clothing of the white upper-middle class. On the other hand, Pilate's outfit is different from the winter coats worn by the rest of the crowd, making her look like an outsider.

Although she is visibly poor, Pilate's attitude demonstrates her strength. When Robert Smith towers over the crowd, only Pilate is brave enough to look him in the eye and respond, singing. Pilate's song describes Robert Smith's frustrated desire to escape. The song also foreshadows the novel's central conflict: flying away is liberating but hurts those who are left behind.

2. He didn't mean it. It happened before he was through. She'd stepped away from him to pick flowers, returned, and at the sound of her footsteps behind him, he'd turned around before he was through. It was becoming a habit—this concentration on things behind him. Almost as though there were no future to be had.

This passage from Chapter 2 references Milkman Dead's alienation from the world and from himself. Milkman accidentally urinates on Lena during a pit stop on a trip to Honoré Island. At a young age, Milkman has inherited Macon Jr.'s mistrustful attitude and spiritual deadness. Although he is only six years old, Milkman already acts like a world-weary man. Milkman's "concentration on things behind him" shows that he is different from other children his age, who have faith in the future. When Milkman turns "at the sound of . . . footsteps behind him," he shows how his father, who fled Pennsylvania after killing a man, has passed to his son the mentality of a hunted man. Milkman's childhood is disfigured by events that took place before his birth. Milkman's alienation is one example of Morrison's argument that a single instance of racism can harm generations of people. Ironically, Milkman's preoccupation with the past eventually allows him to bring closure to the family's suffering by discovering his family history.

This passage also refers to the motif of trauma inflicted by men on women. During the drive to Honoré Island, Milkman urinates on his sister unintentionally. As Lena expresses in Chapter 9, urination becomes a metaphor for Milkman's treatment of his sisters and other women in his life. Milkman is so concerned with his own problems that he doesn't see that he is given special treatment by his family. Milkman is always supported by women behind the scenes: his sisters, Hagar, Pilate, and his mother. He fails, however, to reciprocate their generosity.

3.   Milkman closed his eyes and opened them. The
      street was even more crowded with people, all going
      in the direction he was coming from. All walking
      hurriedly and bumping against him. After a while he
      realized that nobody was walking on the other side of
      the street.

This passage, from Chapter 3, describes Milkman wandering the
streets, distraught about his parents' relationship. As Milkman
begins to face dark moments from his childhood and from his family's past, he also realizes that he is completely alone in his endeavor.
Even Guitar fails to salve his friend's wounds. On the same night
Macon strikes his father and remembers that his mother breast-fed
him through infancy, the rest of the Michigan town discusses the
recent lynching of Emmett Till in Mississippi. Unlike Guitar, who
takes the community's problems too seriously, Milkman is an ego-
tist, concerned only with his own tribulations. Heading against the
flow of traffic, Milkman is not a maverick, but an alien, alone in his
town and unwelcomed by its residents.

This scene occurs at the beginning of Milkman's journey to
uncover his family's past. But from its inception, this journey is different from all other journeys, and puts Milkman at odds with the
rest of humankind. It is also the beginning of the end of Milkman's
childhood. At twenty-two years old, Milkman is beginning to act
like a grown man, capable of handling responsibility. Of course, at
this time Milkman is not yet ready for the full burdens and privileges
of being an adult. Growing up comes at the end of his journey.

QUOTATIONS

4. "Gold," he whispered, and immediately, like a burglar on his first job, stood up to pee.

Life, safety, and luxury fanned out before him like the tailspread of a peacock, and as he stood there trying to distinguish each delicious color, he saw the dusty boots of his father standing just on the other side of the shallow pit.

This quotation, from Chapter 7, describes how Macon Jr. discovers gold treasure in a cave after killing the white man. The quotation describes a crucial turning point in Macon Jr.'s life. Before his father is murdered and before he attempts to kill the white man, Macon Jr. is a simple, kind-hearted farm boy. Macon Dead I's murder, however, ends Macon Jr.'s idyllic childhood. Gold promises a resolution to all of his recent traumas. Finding the gold in the cave is a turning point in Macon's life, after which he believes that wealth will solve his problems. Although he sees the dusty boots of his father standing on the other side of the treasure pit, Macon Jr. does not speak to him, and seems to ignore him altogether. Gold becomes more important than Macon Jr.'s love for the man he cares about most.

The comparison of gold to a "tailspread of a peacock" indicates that the promise of luxury is false. The peacock's tail teases with a temporary display of beauty, and quickly disappears. Likewise, wealth does not heal Macon Jr.'s wounds. Instead, it makes them permanent. The moment that Macon Jr. discovers the gold is the moment when he begins his transformation from hard-working farm boy to soulless landlord.

5.   O Solomon don't leave me here
       Cotton balls to choke me
       O Solomon don't leave me here
       Buckra's arms to yoke me

       Solomon done fly, Solomon done gone
       Solomon cut across the sky, Solomon gone home.

Milkman hears Shalimar children singing these lyrics, a part of Solomon's song, in Chapter 12. The song connects Milkman to his family's past and provides him with crucial stories about his grandfather, Jake, and his great-grandparents, Solomon and Ryna.

Solomon's song implies that when men free themselves from oppression they often leave women behind. "O Solomon don't leave me here" describes Ryna's descent into desperation and madness as Solomon prepares for his flight. Although Solomon escapes slavery, his flight leaves Ryna to take care of their children while working in the cotton fields. The theme of male liberation coming at the expense of female oppression is reflected in Milkman's relationship with Hagar, and recurs throughout Morrison's novel.

Even though Solomon's flight dooms Ryna to abandonment and his children to orphanhood, the song suggests that his flight is still a magnificent achievement. Solomon's song ends with a description of Solomon's flight rather than with a description of Ryna's deprivation. This ending shows the ultimate triumph of liberation. As a result, when Milkman learns that the song is actually about his family, he is not saddened, but inspired. Though tainted by the pain of abandonment, Solomon's flight is an important part of Milkman's heritage. In learning about Solomon's story, Milkman learns pieces of his own, allowing him, finally, to fly free—literally and figuratively.

QUOTATIONS

KEY FACTS

FULL TITLE
Song of Solomon

AUTHOR
Toni Morrison

TYPE OF WORK
Novel

GENRE
Fiction, with elements of magical realism, adventure story, epic, and bildungsroman

LANGUAGE
English

TIME AND PLACE WRITTEN
1977, United States

DATE OF FIRST PUBLICATION
1977

PUBLISHER
Penguin Books

NARRATOR
The novel is told through limited omniscient narration.

POINT OF VIEW
The narrator speaks in the third person, but concentrates at times on what individual characters are thinking, feeling, seeing, and hearing. Because the narrator switches focus from character to character, we know more about the events in the novel than any of the individual characters. While the narrator interprets and comments on the characters' feelings and actions, we do not know whether the narrator's observations are accurate or complete.

TENSE
Past

SETTING (TIME)

Most of the action in the novel takes place between 1931 and 1963, but there are occasional flashbacks reaching as far back as the late nineteenth century.

SETTING (PLACE)

An unnamed city in Michigan (probably Detroit); Pennsylvania; and Virginia.

PROTAGONIST

Critics are divided over who is ultimately the protagonist of Morrison's novel: Milkman Dead (also known as Macon Dead III) or Pilate Dead.

MAJOR CONFLICT

Milkman Dead tries to leave the confines of his parents' home and become an independent man. He is hampered by restrictions of wealth and class, as well as ignorance of his own family history.

RISING ACTION

Stifled by the oppressive conditions of Macon Jr.'s household, Milkman becomes involved in a harebrained scheme to win financial independence by stealing gold from Pilate.

CLIMAX

After traveling from Michigan to Pennsylvania, Milkman finds a cave in which there is supposed to be hidden treasure. After examining the depths of the cave, however, Milkman discovers that there is no treasure after all.

FALLING ACTION

After he fails to find gold in a Pennsylvania cave, Milkman's quest is transformed into a journey of personal self-discovery. Milkman travels to Shalimar, Virginia, where he uncovers his long-lost family history.

THEMES

Flight as a means of escape; abandoned women; the alienating effects of racism

MOTIFS

Biblical allusions; names; singing

SYMBOLS

Whiteness; artificial roses; gold

FORESHADOWING

Milkman's eventual flight off Solomon's Leap is foreshadowed
in the first chapter when we are told that he is born in Mercy
Hospital the day after Robert Smith's flight. The song Pilate
sings in the first chapter, about Sugarman's flight home,
foreshadows the eventual discovery of Solomon's Song in
Shalimar. Guitar's involvement with the Seven Days is
foreshadowed during his heated participation in the discussions
about racism at Tommy's Barbershop. First Corinthians's love
affair with Porter, a member of the Seven Days, is foreshadowed
when Freddie tells Milkman that Guitar might be involved in
covering up a murder of a white boy. Finally, in his statements to
Pilate, the ghost of Macon Dead I reveals both his wife's name,
Sing, and also the fact that his are the bones tied up in the
green bundle.

KEY FACTS

STUDY QUESTIONS & ESSAY TOPICS

STUDY QUESTIONS

1. *Compare and contrast Pilate and Ruth. How does each of them treat Milkman? How does belonging to different economic classes affect their relationship with each other?*

On the surface, no two women in *Song of Solomon* seem more different from each other than Pilate and Ruth. Although Pilate is poor and isolated, she is strong and independent. On the other hand, Ruth is a wealthy, refined, and entirely dependent on her husband. Ruth exchanges her freedom for material possessions. Furthermore, unlike Pilate, Ruth is entirely powerless and unable to change her own life or how others treat her.

These two seemingly different women are bound together by their shared love for Milkman. Pilate and Ruth raise Milkman together. Their concern for Milkman is more important than any boundaries caused by their different social and economic classes. Although Ruth does not befriend any women on the Southside and Pilate never goes to Not Doctor Street, the two women are at ease and open with each other. Through their deep bond, Morrison shows us that a shared love is more important in bringing people together than any superficial markers of status.

2. *Compare and contrast Macon Jr.'s and Milkman's quests for gold. How does searching for gold alter their personalities?*

Although both men seek money, they approach their quests differently. For Macon Jr., gold becomes an end in itself. However, Milkman's quest for financial riches becomes a journey to uncover his family history. Having seen his father die while defending his land, Macon Jr. develops an unhealthy attachment to material things. For example, when Macon Jr. sees gold nuggets in Hunter's Cave after murdering an old white man, his humanity begins to disappear. He neither regrets killing the white man nor pays attention to his father's ghost, who is trying to speak to him. Although he never recovers the gold he sees in Hunter's Cave, Macon Jr. spends his life trying to find the wealth he believes he has lost. He severs the relationship with his sister, Pilate, and damages the relationship with his immediate family, revealing that he does not own his gold. Instead, his gold owns him.

Initially Milkman is just as captivated by gold as his father, Macon Jr. However, Milkman does not seek gold for its own sake. For Milkman, gold is a tool, an instrument that can win him independence from his parents. Because Milkman never becomes as attached to the image of gold as Macon Jr., he is able to let go of his search for gold when his efforts fail. The quest for gold enriches Milkman because it puts him on the path of personal discovery.

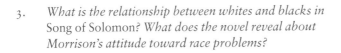

3. *What is the relationship between whites and blacks in* Song of Solomon? *What does the novel reveal about Morrison's attitude toward race problems?*

Song of Solomon's themes are universal, but almost all of its characters are black. We rarely meet any white characters, but we know that an oppressive white world exists just outside the black world. The few times that white characters do enter the novel, the consequences are immediate and devastating. White people in *Song of Solomon* are a source of harm for black people: Macon Dead I is murdered by a wealthy white family, and Guitar's father dies in a factory accident because of his white boss's negligence. Also, Emmett Till is hung in Mississippi by a white lynch mob, and four little girls are killed in a Birmingham church bombing.

Despite the whites' catastrophic presence, Morrison warns that hatred and revenge are not useful responses to racism. Guitar's lust for vengeance eventually causes him to attempt to murder Milkman, a black man just like him. While Morrison understands Guitar's desire for justice in an oppressive white society, she shows that his anger is detrimental to his cause. By focusing on those who hate him rather than on himself, Guitar achieves nothing. Milkman, on the other hand, realizes his individual potential and liberates himself from his personal limitations.

QUESTIONS & ESSAYS

SUGGESTED ESSAY TOPICS

1. How do various genres such as magical realism, adventure story, and heroic epic, typify the plot of the novel? Is one genre term more appropriate than others? If so, why?

2. How does poorness influence participation in the Seven Days? Though the group is motivated by racism rather than economic injustice, why are all its members poor?

3. How is the relationship between love for an individual and love for an ideology explored in the novel? What are the similarities and differences between Hagar's and Guitar's expressions of love?

4. How do physical abnormalities represent the personality traits of the novel's characters? Does Pilate's lack of a navel have the same effect on her as Milkman's undersized leg has on him?

5. What is the ideological agenda embedded in the novel? Is there a moral lesson to be learned from *Song of Solomon*? If so, what is it?

REVIEW & RESOURCES

QUIZ

1. What is Macon Dead I's real name?

    A.   Jake
    B.   Mike
    C.   Jared
    D.   Robert

2. How does Milkman find out his grandfather's and grandmother's names?

    A.   They are inscribed on a piece of paper hidden in Pilate's earring
    B.   Macon Jr. reveals them during a father-son talk
    C.   Circe tells him them
    D.   Susan Byrd finds them on a family tree chart

3. What is inside Pilate's green bundle?

    A.   Gold
    B.   Jake's bones
    C.   The remains of an old white man
    D.   One of Guitar's victims

4. Where does Robert Smith promise to fly?

    A.   The other side of Lake Superior
    B.   Africa
    C.   Shalimar
    D.   Louisiana

5. Where do Macon Jr. and Pilate grow up?

    A.   Shalimar
    B.   Lincoln's Heaven
    C.   The Butler Mansion
    D.   Michigan

6. How does Hagar react after Milkman ends their relationship?

    A. She starts dating Guitar
    B. She joins a convent
    C. She tries to kill Milkman
    D. She blackmails Milkman

7. Where are Jake's remains ultimately buried?

    A. The Hunters' Cave
    B. Solomon's Leap
    C. Africa
    D. Macon, Georgia

8. What does Reba win at Sears Roebuck?

    A. A diamond ring
    B. Dishware
    C. A vacuum cleaner
    D. A dress for Hagar

9. How does Macon Dead I pick names for his children after his firstborn son?

    A. He finds them in a name book
    B. He chooses them at random from the Bible
    C. He lets Circe name them
    D. He asks his wife for suggestions

10. Who is First Corinthians's secret lover?

    A. Guitar
    B. Robert Smith
    C. Omar
    D. Henry Porter

11. Why is Macon Jr. angry with Ruth?

    A. He thinks she had an affair with her father, Dr. Foster
    B. He believes Ruth acts as though she is superior to him
    C. He thinks that Ruth abuses their daughters
    D. He thinks that Ruth wants to kill him

12. How old is Milkman when he strikes his father, Macon Jr.?

    A.   22
    B.   24
    C.   16
    D.   32

13. Why does Guitar want to kill Milkman?

    A.   Because Milkman abused his beloved Hagar
    B.   Because Guitar is jealous of Milkman's wealth
    C.   Because Guitar thinks that Milkman has stolen gold to which he, Guitar, is entitled
    D.   Because Milkman constantly invades his privacy

14. In what year does *Song of Solomon* open?

    A.   1942
    B.   1926
    C.   1963
    D.   1931

15. How does Guitar try to kill Milkman in his first attempt?

    A.   By strangling him with a wire
    B.   By holding his face underwater
    C.   By shooting him in the abdomen
    D.   By stabbing him in the shoulder

16. To what town is Lincoln's Heaven closest?

    A.   Shalimar, Virginia
    B.   Macon, Georgia
    C.   Pittsburgh, Pennsylvania
    D.   Danville, Pennsylvania

17. To what secret organization does Guitar belong?

    A.   The Ku Klux Klan
    B.   The Masons
    C.   The Seven Days
    D.   The Elks

18. From which college does First Corinthians receive her degree?

    A. Spelman
    B. Howard
    C. Bryn Mawr
    D. Wellesley

19. What is unusual about Pilate's body?

    A. She has no eyebrows
    B. She has no fingernails
    C. She has no big toe
    D. She has no navel

20. How old is Ruth when she marries Macon Dead II?

    A. 16
    B. 19
    C. 25
    D. 11

21. What is the official name of Not Doctor Street?

    A. Doctor Street
    B. Buckra Boulevard
    C. Cleveland Circle
    D. Mains Avenue

22. Who is the first black child born in Mercy Hospital?

    A. Robert Smith
    B. First Corinthians Dead
    C. Magdalene Dead
    D. Milkman Dead

23. Whom does Solomon try to take with him when he flies back to Africa?

    A. Jake
    B. Ryna
    C. Circe
    D. Pilate

24. Why does Circe stay in the Butlers' mansion after they die?

    A. She wants to see it rot away
    B. She wants to enjoy a life of luxury
    C. She is waiting for the return of Solomon
    D. She wants to preserve it as a memorial to the Butlers

25. What does Grace Long give to Milkman when he leaves?

    A. Her watch
    B. Her phone number
    C. A box of cookies
    D. A new pair of boots

SUGGESTIONS FOR FURTHER READING

BERKMAN, ANNE ELIZABETH. *The Quest for Authenticity: The Novels of Toni Morrison.* Ann Arbor: UMI, 1987.

CARMEAN, KAREN. *Toni Morrison's World of Fiction.* Troy, New York: The Whitson Publishing Company, 1993.

CONNER, MARC C. *The Aesthetics of Toni Morrison: Speaking the Unspeakable.* Jackson: University Press of Mississippi, 2000.

DAVID, RON. *Toni Morrison Explained.* New York: Random House, 2000.

KUBITSCHEK, MISSY DEHN. *Toni Morrison: A Critical Companion.* Westport, Connecticut: Greenwood Press, 1988.

MATUS, JILL. *Toni Morrison.* New York: St. Martin's Press, 1998.

MCKAY, NELLIE Y. and KATHRYN EARLE, eds. *Approaches to Teaching the Novels of Toni Morrison.* New York: The Modern Language Association of America, 1997.

PEACH, LINDEN. *Toni Morrison.* New York: St. Martin's Press, 2000.

SMITH, VALERIE. *New Essays on* SONG OF SOLOMON. Cambridge: Cambridge University Press, 1995.

SUMANA, K. *The Novels of Toni Morrison: A Study in Race, Gender, and Class.* London: Sangam Books, 1998.

SPARKNOTES
TEST PREPARATION
GUIDES

The SparkNotes team figured it was time to cut standardized tests down to size. We've studied the tests for you, so that SparkNotes test prep guides are:

Smarter:
Packed with critical-thinking skills and test-
taking strategies that will improve your score.

Better:
Fully up to date, covering all new features of the tests,
with study tips on every type of question.

Faster:
Our books cover exactly what you need to
know for the test. No more, no less.

SparkNotes Study Guides: